Child Labour in Jamaica

Child Labour in Jamaica
A General Review

Judith Ennew and Pansy Young

Anti-Slavery Society
Child Labour Series
Report No 6 – 1981

© 1981 Anti-Slavery Society

Published by Anti-Slavery Society
180 Brixton Road
London SW9 6AT

Printed by Calverts North Star Press Ltd
Typeset by Dessett Graphics Limited

ISBN 0 900918 11 X

Judith Ennew trained at the University of Cambridge, is a freelance consultative anthropologist, and has conducted research on the impact of oil-related industry in the Scottish Highlands. She is the author of *The Western Isles Today* and of the Anti-Slavery Society report, *Debt Bondage – A Survey*.

Pansy Young is a Jamaican schoolteacher who has been involved in research into handicapped children in schools, language teaching materials and pre-school services in Jamaica. She is co-author of 'A Project for the Handicapped' published in *Torch*, Journal of the Ministry of Education, Jamaica.

Map by Vicky Ram
Drawings by Jamaican schoolchildren

Average rate of exchange
February to April 1980: £1 = Jam $3.75

Contents

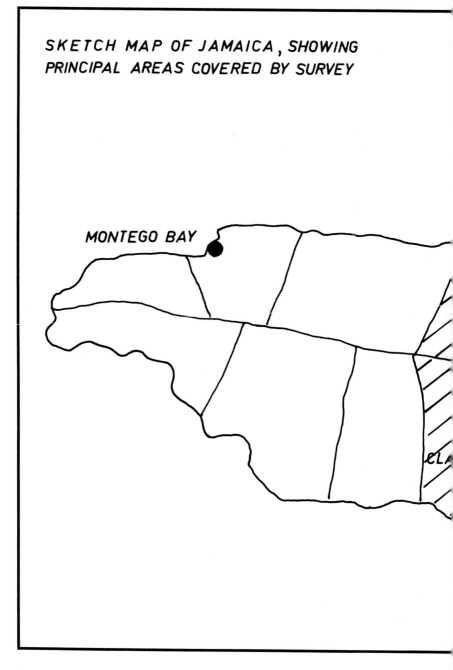

SKETCH MAP OF JAMAICA, SHOWING
PRINCIPAL AREAS COVERED BY SURVEY

MONTEGO BAY

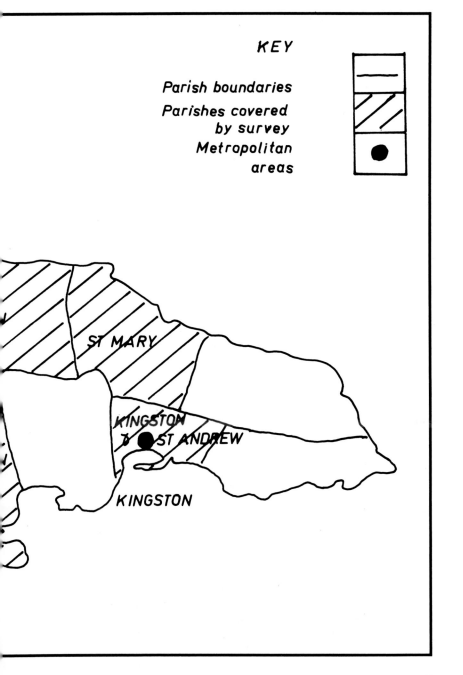

KEY

Parish boundaries
Parishes covered
by survey
Metropolitan
areas

ST MARY

KINGSTON & ST ANDREW

KINGSTON

7

Acknowledgements

The authors wish to express their gratitude to those members of staff at the University of the West Indies, Mona Campus, who were so generous with their time and advice, particularly Dr Erna Brodber and Mrs Dorian Powell of the Institute of Social and Economic Research, to which the project was affiliated. In addition, we should particularly like to thank Mrs Sylvan Alleyne, Miss Meta Bogle, Dr Barry Chevannes, Miss June Dolly-Besson, Mrs Sybil Francis, Mrs Winnie Hewitt, Dr Errol Miller and his staff, Professors Reid and Phillips of the Department of Education and Miss Jean Tulloch-Read. We are grateful for the co-operation of numerous individuals, in various organisations and government departments, particularly in the Child Care and Protection Division of the Ministry of Health, the Council for Voluntary Social Services, the Family Court, JAMAL (Jamaican Movement for the Advancement of Literacy), the Ministry of Education, the National Planning Institute, the Social Development Commission, VOUCH (Voluntary Organisation for the Upliftment of Children) and the Women's Bureau. Our particular thanks go to Edwin Jorge and Owen Sullivan of the Trafalgar Street Boys' Project for help, information and friendship. Back in England, Colin Duly was unfailingly helpful with the computer programming.

Most importantly, we should like to thank the principals, teachers and pupils of the Jamaican schools we visited, for making us so welcome in the middle of busy working days. This report is dedicated to the children of Jamaica, but particularly to those whose words and pictures we have used. The words are taken either from essays written for us or from tape-recorded interviews, and we have retained the original spellings and creole syntax, partly to illustrate the widespread use of Jamaican creole. With the exception of pictures 1 and 2 the drawings were made by primary school children in grades 1-3 (ages five to seven) to illustrate what they did during the time when they were not at school. The other two pictures were drawn by secondary school boys, both aged fifteen. Individual schools, principals, teachers and pupils as well as the names of some other informants are not identified in this report. Most of the information we received was subject to promises of confidentiality which we were concerned to respect. Nevertheless, we intend to deposit the original research data in the library of the Institute of Social and Economic Research (ISER), University of the West Indies, where, with due provision for safeguarding confidentiality, it will be available to other researchers.

The research undertaken included an analysis of the social and economic aspects of child labour which falls outside the scope of this publication. But a subsequent report by the Anti-Slavery Society will incorporate these data.

Preface

'Most children idle their time away when they are not in school. Some children study in every time they have got. While some children work, work, work.'

(12-year-old Jamaican boy)

In Jamaica, manufacture, agriculture and tourism are the three principle sectors of the formal economy within which child labour might be found. But, as will become clear in this report, it is the informal or casual sector of the economy which exhibits the highest incidence of child labour. It was primarily for this reason that the island was chosen as a research area. Although there have been some excellent reports on particular examples of exploitation in specific industries or enterprises within the formal sector in other countries, most of the world's working children work in the informal sector and in agriculture. In the case of the formal economy, specific legislation and provisions can be made against the use of child labour, and formal legal action can be prepared or taken although it cannot always be implemented.

But where a child is engaged in working within the informal structures of the economy, the reasons why it is working, the hours worked, the degree of damage which is done to its future opportunities, even the quantification of the incidence of such labour are all less tangible. It is even more difficult to apportion the blame for 'exploitation'. A child may be self-employed in a family enterprise in which the skills learned are of more relevance to obtaining an income as an adult than the skills which night be imparted in an education system. How can these be described as exploitation and who is to blame? It is difficult to locate a primary cause without lapsing into loosely formulated attacks upon widely-defined entities like 'capitalism', 'imperialism' and 'transnational corporations'. Legislation, however well intentioned, cannot compensate for an economic situation which makes it imperative for a child to work.

11

This report should therefore be viewed simply as an attempt to describe and quantify the ways in which children work in a small nation state which is politically independent but economically dependent. It is hoped that the information offered and the conclusions may be useful for understanding similar situations in other places, for the formulation of further research projects and strategies, as well as for those who make policy decisions.

The main period of fieldwork lasted from February to April 1980. This was, as it happened, a time of some disruption in Jamaica. The start of fieldwork coincided with Prime Minister Michael Manley's announcement that a general election would be held, because negotiations with the International Monetary Fund (IMF), over a loan, had broken down. The country was in the grip of economic hardship and political controversy, and we were conscious of an accentuation of certain aspects of the patterns we discovered. Since the General Election of November 1980 Jamaica has had a new Prime Minister, Edward Seaga, who leads the Jamaica Labour Party. Early in 1981 Mr Seaga negotiated successfully with the IMF for loans totalling over £600 million but, at the time of writing this report, there had as yet been no major improvements in economic conditions for the majority of Jamaica's two million people.

1 The Context

Extract from an interview with thirteen-year-old 'Henry', a Jamaican street worker.

Q. How many in your family, Henry?
A. I caan count the names, but there's five in the family that live down the yard now.

Q. How many brothers and sisters do you have altogether?
A. Three sisters and six brothers.

Q. Who's the eldest?
A. My big brother, name Paul.

Q. And his age?
A. Twenty.

Q. And the youngest?
A. My little brother, name Carl, nine year old.

Q. And how old's your mother?
A. Thirty-five. My other brother who is in Miami with my mother is eighteen. My mother live in Miami, Florida.

Q. So you live with your father. What type of work does your father do?
A. Building work.

Q. Do you know how much money he makes?
A. Some time him do a day work him get all of fifty dollar, thirty dollar, forty dollar.

Q. And he feeds everybody with that money?
A. Yes.

Q. Why aren't you in school this morning?
A. Well mi school clothe never get fe wash in de week, because mi did

gone out and hustle. After mi come from school Tuesday, school neva keep Wednesday, Thursday and Friday an mi caan go. Hustle Saturday and Sunday. Neva get fe wash it an mi father gone out.

Q. What type of hustling do you do?

A. Clean car glass [windscreens] an sell *Star* [newspaper], an wash car.

Q. And how much money do you make in a good day?

A. Sometime I mek eight dollar . . . an five dollar.

Q. And how many *Stars* do you buy to sell?

A. I don' buy them, ther's a man give us some fe sell for 'im.

Q. And how much does he give you?

A. 'Im give me fifty *Star* an' give me dollar twenty.

Q. What do you do with the money?

A. I mek it up wi' what mi hustle an' den go roun' an' spend a dollar out ot it an' give my father [the rest]; an' if I have five dollar give father three dollar and tek one dollar t'school.

Q. Is there a lot of fighting on the street corners?

A. Yes, some time. Some time the boy dem always come tek wey mi money; an' when mi no gi'dem wan' come mi an lik mi wi' stone. An' one day, some way up at de corner right dere, an' mi have dollar fifty eena mi pocket, an'a boy name Country tek out de dollar fifty and den 'im tek wey fifty cent an' gimme back de dollar. Mi start to cry an' den a lady gimme thirty cent, an' a white man was passin' an' im go round de corner an' 'im come roun' back an gimme dollar.

Q. Do all the boys carry knives?

A. Not all of dem, som'a dem break bottle an' cut you wid it.

Q. What do you want to be when you grow up?

A. I like to be a engineer; fix plane an' ship, train, all sorts of ting.

Q. And what will that do for you?

A. That I can feed myself, rent a room an' 'ave a wife.

Q. If I could give you anything you want in the world, what would you ask me for?

A. (pause) Education, a pants and a shirt.

The interviewer and interviewee sit in a dusty room on the top floor of the decaying YMCA building in the centre of Kingston. Heat and glaring light pour through the open shutters and one can hear the constant roar of traffic outside, as cars stop for the lights of the busy Trafalgar intersection, where 'Henry' works. The room is almost bare of equipment, for this aid programme is run on a small budget, and may

14

have to stop when funds run out in a fortnight's time. On the blackboard, above a few, simple sums, uneven letters chalk the programme's unofficial slogan: 'Respect yourself, or no-one else will'.

The boy is small for his age, covered in dust from the road where he has been dodging cars all morning. He wears a tattered man's shirt, old trousers cut down to shorts and no shoes. His hands, which dangle between his bare knees, keep a firm, but unconscious, grasp on the dirty rag, which is the tool of his trade as windscreen wiper. He is wary, even his trust for the programme's staff members, built up gradually over three months, is precarious.

This interview, chosen almost at random from a series made for us by this programme's staff, reveals the conditions in which this boy and his fellow street workers live and work – conditions which, as our report will show, are experienced to a greater or lesser degree, by thousands of Jamaican children, forcing them to work for much of their 'childhood' and denying them the physical conditions and educational provision, through which they might be able to fulfil their potential in adulthood.

Shortly after this interview was recorded, the Trafalgar Street Boys' project received further funds from the Canadian High Commission, enabling work to continue for another year. We will describe this work later in this report. But there are many children like Henry in Jamaica, who have not yet been helped by projects like this; children who are semi-independent, sometimes because of their position in a loose-knit family structure; children whose education is scanty or virtually non-existent, because of lack of parental encouragement, poor school facilities, necessity to work, or lack of money for school uniform; children whose parents or guardians are unemployed or work in the informal sector.

Henry's own aspirations are modest, because he has become accustomed to seeking short-term gains. Indeed his long-term prospects as an adult are poor, and he is likely to become, at best, a casual worker, like his father, existing on the income of an occasional day's employment. It may be that an adequate subsistence income, a reasonable home and a wife will all elude Henry. The reasons for this are to be found in the social and economic structure of Jamaica, which we shall now briefly examine, before going on to explore further the situation of other Jamaican child workers, in the street and elsewhere.

Economic Background

The Jamaican economy is based on private enterprise and an important element is foreign participation, both as direct investment and in the form of aid. The dominant elements now are bauxite mining, manufacturing and tourism, but the history of the island is that of monoculture and plantation economy. More than 25 per cent of the regular wage labour force is involved in agriculture and 46 per cent is employed in services and administration (1977 *Abstract of Statistics*, Government of Jamaica, Kingston). The manufacturing sector is not firmly based in local resources and has a weak structure which particularly makes it vulnerable to fluctuations in external markets. During the time of fieldwork this sector was collapsing, because of a lack of foreign exchange for importing raw materials. The past few years have seen a polarisation of political views within the country and reports that considerable amounts of local capital have been withdrawn by small businessmen who have emigrated to North America. Early in 1980, local newspapers estimated that at least 50 per cent of local manufacturing enterprises closed down because of the lack of raw materials (*Daily Gleaner; Star;* Kingston, various editions, March 1980). This caused increased shortages of essential foods and household items in shops, exacerbated black market trading and worsened the unemployment problem.

The activities of transnational companies, such as those involved in bauxite mining (Alcan and Reynolds (Jamaica) Mines, for example), have increased the gross domestic product (GDP) of the country, but failed to catalyse self-sustaining growth. Since independence in 1962, the country has become increasingly dependent on United States and Canadian capital. Although labour productivity and wage rates in the bauxite industry are high, it is capital intensive and, as the bulk of Jamaican bauxite is exported unprocessed, the total labour force and the overall wage bill are relatively low.

In Jamaica the stable area of employment is within the capital-intensive, foreign-financed industry. But in the early months of 1980, as the economy faced collapse because of international debt and a dearth of foreign exchange, unemployment became endemic and the casual sector increased to unmanageable proportions.

Jamaica is also characterised by a very high degree of class distinction. A small wealthy minority, largely lightskinned, lives in style and comfort and controls access to education and employment. Many of the poor majority live in remote rural areas or urban slums, both of which lack many basic amenities. To a large extent, the parents of the children we studied were poorly housed and not in regular wage employment. As 40 to 50 per cent of adult Jamaicans are illiterate (JAMAL Foundation, Kingston 1980) the children tended to come from educationally disadvantaged homes.

One of the main reasons for selecting Jamaica as a research area was the size of the unemployment problem. As the country has only a rudimentary social welfare programme and does not possess sufficient resources to increase this provision, a large casual sector has long been a feature of the economy. The unemployed adopt a number of strategies to ensure their survival as well as that of their dependents. One of these strategies is to ensure that all possible household members obtain an income. Certain groups are particularly vulnerable to exploitation within the casual sector because they are unable to take up the few opportunities for regular wage labour. Some are prevented by social circumstance and others by legislation. Thus the core of the casual sector is formed by women with young children, the very old, the disabled, the unskilled and illiterate and, of course, children.

The income obtained from sending children out to work can be regarded as an addition to the savings from not sending them to school, for which the Jamaican education system requires substantial outlay on school uniforms and equipment. We found that considerable numbers of children were involved in casual labour, which we understood as encompassing a wide variety of income-generating activities or ways of making a living, all of which lie outside the recognised or legitimate sphere of employment. Much of this casual labour could be prevented and not all could be considered to be a necessary contribution to household income.

In the course of the study, we isolated three factors which affect the situation in Jamaica and which operate within the general situation of political instability and economic collapse. These three factors, unemployment, education and family structure, should be regarded as a background to the description of child labour in this report.

Unemployment
Like the high rate of emigration to which it is linked, high unemployment has always been a crucial element in Jamaican economic history. Recent estimates indicate levels of over 30 per cent and an even wider incidence of under-employment (*Daily Gleaner*, Kingston, 16 March 1980). Within certain age groups, particularly young people, the incidence is even higher. For girls in the 17 to 24 age group living in the metropolitan area, unemployment has been reported to be over 60 per cent (see also Figure 1). When children in their early teens see such poor employment prospects in the immediate future, there is little incentive to stay at school unless they can anticipate further education and a white-collar job. Thus many children under school leaving age drop out and join their parents or peer group in the casual sector.

Under the National Insurance Scheme, which was established in 1966, certain gainfully employed persons over the age of 18 can obtain unemployment benefit, and certain benefits are available, for example, to widows and old people. But the National Insurance Scheme was not intended to provide complete social protection. There is a non-contributory Public Assistance Scheme, which enables heads of families to claim a small subsistence payment. But the sums involved are inadequate and there is a limit on the period during which payments can be made. Henry's father, earning the occasional 30 to 50 dollars would be unable to claim and, as a casual worker, would not be eligible for the National Insurance Scheme.

The Jamaican unemployment problem therefore has three immediate effects on Jamaican children. It means that they are aware of their meagre prospects of future employment in the formal sector and this encourages them to seek work, often while still of school age, in the casual sector. It means that their immediate family often does not live in the same household, or even in the same country, because of the necessity for adults to seek work away from home. And it means that the income provided by adults to that home is often insufficient to provide for the subsistence of all household members.

Education

Children like Henry have often dropped out of school or are not regular attenders. Sometimes this is not entirely due to the necessity to work, but is related to the unsuitability of the education system for children from poor social and economic backgrounds.

The education system is based on the English system, in the form it took before Jamaican independence in 1962. By philosophy, it is a three tier system. Children enter primary school at five years of age and take an examination at grade 6 (aged 11), which can give them the opportunity, if they pass, for an academic education in a high school. The alternative is a more practical education in a secondary school. There is a second chance to obtain a place at a high school by taking an examination at grade 9. If they fail this, then they have the opportunity of staying at school for two extra years and following a course which has a technical, employment-oriented basis and which includes work experience.

Despite this philosophy, two other historical elements characterise the system. The first is the all-age school, which has often been described as the backbone of the system, particularly in rural areas. This offers children an education from grades 1 to 9, with the chance of gaining one of the prized high school places at 11 or 15 years old. Because all-age schools have a better reputation for passes at the 'Grade 9 Examination', many parents prefer to send their children to this type of school, rather than to a secondary school, after an 11-plus failure.

The second factor is the existence of a large private sector in education. Without this, the public sector would be unable to function at its present level. Needless to say, therefore, that the education a child receives is strongly related to its social class position, even within the public sector. The strain on resources in public sector schools can be judged from the fact that many primary and secondary schools operate a shift system in order to accommodate the number of children eligible for education.

School attendance is affected by unemployment. If children can foresee no secure future employment, there can seem little need to remain at school to obtain paper qualifications which will not help to get a better job, for they are aware that no such job exists. Parental and peer group pressures may encourage children to leave school early and join the growing labour force of drop-outs who can earn quite large incomes within the casual sector. Dropping out usually takes place from 10 to 12 years of age, particularly among boys who have failed the 11-plus and are big enough to generate a reasonable income by street vending, begging, pilfering and in petty service industries – an activity known in Jamaica by the generic term 'hustling'.

Absenteeism is also a critical problem, particularly in rural areas, where regular employment prospects are very low indeed. Children frequently miss school in order to help on family farms or in preparing a load for market. In all areas, Friday is a day of particularly poor attendance partly because it was previously not a school day (Figure 2). It may be that an addition to the family labour force is necessary, but this is not always the case. Parents are reported as 'seeing no value' in school attendance, particularly for non-academic children. They will thus keep children away from school for a variety of reasons, which are not always connected to the necessity for extra labour in a household enterprise (Figures 3 and 4). Five per cent of our main sample of school children complained spontaneously that their parents kept them home when they would rather be at school. One eleven-year-old urban child summed up the reasons why she might be absent from school:

> When I do not come to school, I have to wash the dishes and sweep the yard. Sometimes my mother is sick and I have to look after the little ones. Sometimes I do not feel well. When I am absent from school sometime I was coming and it got late and I just stay home. There is no money sometime then my mother dont send me to school.

Our evidence on absenteeism from 16 schools, seems to concur with the findings of an education ministry research project that it is at its worst in rural areas. Metropolitan areas seem to have the best rates of attendance, but there are variations between schools within Kingston with lower rates in secondary schools in slum areas. Moreover, these figures do not take into account those children who do not enrol in school at all, or who drop out between one school year and the next. In 1979, the author of a booklet prepared for the National Union of Democratic Teachers stated:

> Today no less than 250,000 youths (or 33 per cent) between the ages of 6-18 years are not enrolled in or attending school. This can be broken down as follows:
> – in the 6-11 year age group 10.8 per cent are out of school
> – in the 12-15 year age group 31.6 per cent are out of school
> – in the 16-18 year age group 81.8 per cent are out of school
> (J Houghton, *A Commonsense Look at Education in Jamaica Today* 1979).

These figures were obtained from those projected in a Ministry of Education report, but in general such reports do not acknowledge the existence or extent of problems. There is what one Jamaican educationist calls an 'atmosphere of unreality' about official statements on education (J Figueroa, *Education, Schools and Progress in the Caribbean*, Pergamon Press, 1971, p.62). If the reports were relied upon, the education system would appear to function as a mirror image of its imagined English counterpart and model. This ideological construction of the education system is authoritarian and to a very large extent inflexible, adjusting only slowly and recently to the realities of the Jamaican situation. The system of teaching is teacher-centred and based essentially upon learning by rote. Text books in many schools are still more suitable in language and subject matter for English schools. The medium of instruction is standard English which, even in its Jamaican variation, is not the familiar language of the home for many creole-speaking children, particularly those in rural and slum areas. Young children from creole-speaking backgrounds may be at a disadvantage by failing to understand instructions and information given to them in school. They will also find it difficult to learn to read from manuals which use unfamiliar words, grammar and rules of pronunciation. Teacher training is not always imaginative and the intake of student teachers is remarkably low in elementary skills of literacy and numeracy. For many children, therefore, school must seem an alien environment and education must appear to be at best irrelevant and at worst totally impenetrable.

Few schools operate efficient guidance and follow-up systems for truancy, absenteeism and persistent lateness. The standard of record-keeping is, in most cases, so low that no check can be made on the welfare, progress and educational standards of the shifting child population. Teachers in some schools simply fail to prepare lessons for Fridays, when large numbers of children stay away.

Teachers are themselves hampered by the authoritarian nature of the system. Yet there is also frustration among administrative personnel despite the complacency of education ministry reports. The 10 changes of education minister during the past nine years reflects a certain amount of instability at the Cabinet level of the 1972-80 Government. Each change has brought about new plans, or variations upon old ones, as well as reversals of philosophy. But no recent minister has held the office for long enough to implement his or her plans properly and this has resulted in dissatisfactions and resignations among civil servants, so that continuity is at risk. The problem is less maladministration than multifarious administration. In the resultant confusion, civil servants fume and teachers grumble, but it is the children who suffer.

Family Structure
The majority of the population lives in one of three household patterns. The grandmother-headed household, first described by anthropologist Edith Clark in her book *My Mother who Fathered Me* (Allen and Unwin, London, 1957) is one form. These households can also be described as consanguineal, as they consist of three generations joined by bonds of blood and kinship. In its typical form, this household would contain a maternal grandmother, her daughter under 25 and her daughter's child or children by one or more non-resident fathers. The father's interest in the household can vary from being a casual, biological progenitor to being a regular visitor who provides some maintenance.

The second alternative is a conjugal, consensual union between a man and a woman, in which the household may also include children of either or both partners from previous unions as well as children of the present nuclear family. But it should be noted that a woman may leave existing children with her mother when she enters a conjugal partnership and that the man may never have had his offspring living with him. Conjugal unions may lead to eventual marriage but conjugal partners may leave to set up new consensual unions which produce more children.

The third alternative is the female-headed single-parent household which may eventually extend, through the generations, to become a grandmother-headed household. Some women choose this alternative, thinking that it has more continuity than the spurious security of a consensual union. There is thus a constellation of blood relations who may be involved, at one time or another, in parenting a particular child. These include grandparents, parents, aunts, uncles and even older siblings. In addition, stepfathers, stepmothers and a variety of step-siblings, as well as relations 'in law', or in fact, but not in blood, may be incorporated into the household. Both fostering and unofficial adoption are common. It is not unusual for one or both parents to migrate to another area, or even overseas, leaving a child in the care of a

21

grandmother, aunt of friend.

The result of this fluid family structure is a shifting population of children which is difficult for the state to administer. It also creates a situation in which some children lack the protection of one or both biological parents. The state does not possess sufficient resources of finance or personnel to undertake the parental role in all such cases and such children are particularly vulnerable to exploitation. Under these circumstances, children learn to think of themselves as independent proto-adults, and the inferior status which they are accorded in a school system orientated towards English traditions, becomes less and less relevant to their self-image.

2 How Many Children Work?

In 1979, the *World Atlas of the Child* (published by the World Bank) reported that roughly one Jamaican child (aged fourteen and under) in every thousand was involved in the labour force and that this figure was expected to drop to 0.2 per thousand by the year 2000. Given these low figures and confident predictions, Jamaica would seem to be an unlikely choice for a study of child labour. But these statistics refer only to the number of children employed as wage labour; they do not include children who obtain an income in the casual sector. In addition, our sample of 2,146 children who attended school, showed 25 clear cases of children in regular wage employment. This is a rate of 11.6 per thousand which does not take into account those children who do not attend school at all, perform part-time and holiday work, or engage in informal apprenticeships.

The Juveniles Act (1951 as amended to 1975) governs the employment of juveniles. No child under 12 can be employed other than by its parents provided that this does not involve work at night or in an industrial undertaking. The minimum age for employment is 15; for night work it is 16.

In practice legislation cannot always be implemented because of the socio-economic realities and inadequacies in infrastructure. Furthermore there is also a contradiction in the legislative provisions: 16 is the school leaving age in Jamaica but 15 is the minimum age for employment. In effect the school leaving age is only a mandatory stipulation, because there is no real provision for truant control, nor indeed are there sufficient educational resources to provide for the number of children entitled to schooling. As we have seen, rates of absenteeism are high, and drop-out rates, particularly among boys in the 10 to 14 age group, are similarly large. Moreover there is a sizeable group of children who never enrol in school at all. Thus it is not surprising that official Jamaican employment figures reflect a group of regular wage earners in the 14 to 19 age group. As can be seen in Figure 5, the number employed in this age group showed a slight increase between 1977 and 1978, despite the fact that young people bear the brunt of the unemployment problem.

In the Anti-Slavery Society's research sample of over 2,000 school children 32 per cent did some work (Fig 6). The vast majority of these were engaged in domestic or household labour, including agricultural work.

Four hundred and fifty-five children, 69 per cent of those working, were involved in activities which either added to the household income, or made it possible for some other member of the household to perform external wage labour. Of the remaining working children, 7.6 per cent were working as informal apprentices, 5.6 per cent were involved in street labour, 3.89 per cent in shops or manufacturing and 1.09 per cent were in fishing. In addition, 7 per cent had part time or holiday jobs and 3 per cent said simply that they worked. Their essays consisted of the scrawled words, 'What I do when I am not at school, I go to work'.

Thus, in the known cases, only a small proportion are engaged in regular wage labour and many of these are involved in part-time or holiday work which fall outside the main interests of this report. Children are mostly engaged in casual work which may best be described as strategies for obtaining cash rather than employment. As we shall show in the next section, many children work, not to generate cash incomes for themselves, but to help in the reproduction of the means of household subsistence. Our main concerns with respect to this type of labour are the extent to which it is necessary, the degree of damage or hardship it inflicts upon a child, and the possibility of improving state provision for such children, given the present economic problems of Jamaica. We shall also present further data, which we feel are insufficiently represented in our sample, concerning child street workers because these are the children who tend not to go to school at all.

3 What Do Children Do?

The Formal Sector

Casual labour escalates in a situation of high unemployment, but even child employment in the formal sector is closely related to adult unemployment. As stated earlier, the brunt of the unemployment problem is borne by the 14 to 24 age group. In some countries, such high levels of unemployment lead to an extension of formal education. Children remain at school longer in order to gain higher qualifications. In Jamaica, however, education success is elusive for many children and the education system can appear irrelevant to a working class child and its family. If regular wage opportunity presents itself, it will seem to be a more attractive proposition. The essays revealed a great deal of anxiety about the future on the part of children who were actively seeking employment. One 15-year-old boy expressed teenage anxiety about the job situation:

> When I am not in school I am going to do a trade they call automechanic because I love that work it is my life time work. I will kill myself for that work because when I leave school I am going to get that job so I can get money to buy food and a house to live in a food to eat and ful my belly. This will help to get myself out of troubles in Jamaica . . . Some people steel when they leave school but I am not going to do those things. I am going to do that job.

Another 16-year-old stated his career preferences as simply 'to go an work for my money'. As a girl of the same age wrote, those with a job 'don't have to sit at home and stared in their mothers face'. Many children wrote of the fear that, without a job, they would be forced to turn to crime. As the same girl expressed it:

> Some of us go out and try to seek jobs because its very hard no nowadays, you cant find anything for yourself. Some of them that are not in school go out and steal people things some of them turn rasta (Rastafarian) and dont know anything in life.

26

Regular work opportunities are therefore highly prized and much sought after. Many are obtained for the older children by parental influence and some children work alongside a relative. Most of this work starts as a part-time or holiday job which children will attempt to fit in with the school day. This may be possible if the school they attend operates a shift system. It is a common observation that children attend the afternooon shift more sporadically than the morning shift, although our own data does not appear to confirm this. However, teachers frequently remarked that children would fail to come to the afternoon session because they were tired after working all morning, or because their work duties had made them late.

Shops and manufacturing

Shops and supermarkets are one source of employment and they may advertise directly for younger children. A 13-year-old Kingston girl wrote, 'One day I saw an advertisement in the paper asking for a school girl about 13-14 to work in a store by dusting the furniture I apply for the job and I got it'. A 15-year-old urban boy stated, 'on Friday evening and Saturdays I go to work at the Phillips supermarket my work is taking baggage from the customers my pay is five dollars per day'. Sometimes such work is available daily. In Kingston a 14-year-old boy wrote, 'In the morning I go to work and come to school in the afternoon. I work in a supermarket and I work in were (where) they take the bag. I go to work 9 O clock and left 11.30'. He also worked all day on Saturday.

In tourist areas, it is possible to fit a full day's schooling around a virtually full-time job, as in the case of a 16-year-old aspiring chef, who worked every evening between 5 pm and 11.30 pm as well as at weekends.

Other teenagers are able to obtain part-time work in offices and one boy in our sample had been able to find work in a library. Despite the many factories which had closed or were on short time during the early part of 1980 children, like the following Kingston boys, could still obtain employment in manufacturing:

(a) 'I work part-time at a spice Company during the week'
(b) 'When I get midterm holiday I work when I say work I mean employ at a factory. I work from Monday to Saturday the work what I do is help fix sewing machine an the only day I get is Sunday.'

It was also reported to us that some 15- and 16-year-olds were working in sugar manufacture and that some would only take time off from work to attend school for the activities they enjoyed, such as sports day. But these youths were not employed in the heavy work in the sugar boiling process as far as we could ascertain. They were apparently engaged in less arduous packing tasks.

Another type of employment, which verges on the borderline between formal and informal employment, is outworking. In many countries with high adult unemployment, outworking among children is a marked feature of some industries, for example, the leather industry in Italy. (See the Anti-Slavery Society's *Child Labour in Italy*, London, 1981). We enquired into this in Jamaica, but there seems to be little evidence of outworking except in the shoe trade. Several boys mentioned making shoes, like the Kingston boy, aged 15, who stated that when he did not attend school 'I stay home and make shoe with my brother in law' (by which he may have meant step-brother).

Although it was reported to us that, in one area, 14-year-olds were employed on construction sites, we did not obtain any direct evidence of this. Nevertheless it is possible that children of that age, or younger, could hang around building sites in the hope of being able to earn the odd dollar by running errands or helping to carry loads. As will be seen later, when we discuss what we call 'multiple labour', one strategy adopted by many children is to keep an eye open for any opportunity to earn money in small amounts. In this case the employment is best described as casual, even though it is associated with sources of regular employment. Our impression was that most of the work mentioned by children in ships and manufacturing was probably casual labour, in that the child would not be put on the payroll. Although many children were clearly working for pocket money and not endangering health or education, the very fact that they are paid as casual labour rather than being taken on as regular employees, renders them particularly liable to exploitation. We heard of cases of children working part-time who did not receive any recompense for their labour, or who received it only sporadically. Besides the absence of any guarantees of payment, the rate for the task may be inadequate. Yet these workers are not protected by trades unions with respect to either pay or conditions. Their employment, which may provide a considerable part of their own means of subsistence, can be terminated without notice and without adequate recompense, and they have no access to state social security under these circumstances. Yet some of these children clearly do regard their employment as regular work.

> When I am not in school I went (go) to the boxing Gem (gym) to work and earn money. every morning When I get up I go to the Gem before the boas (boxers) came. When I go to the Gem if I dont clean out the Gem before the traner or the boxer came they will have to wait until it clean (14-year-old Kingston boy).

Apprentices

The group most liable to exploitation in this sector are the children, mostly boys, whom we designated 'apprentices'. According to the 1977 *Abstract of Statistics* (Government of Jamaica, Kingston) there are 130 to 140 registered, indentured apprentices in any one year. These youths sign contracts for periods of three to eight years with specific employers. At the end of the apprenticeship they should have become competent in a specific craft or skill. But our research was not concerned with these formal situations. The apprentices to which we refer are almost all found in urban situations and overwhelmingly in the metropolitan area (Figure 8). Often they are not even called apprentices and in many cases they are not trained at all, simply kept as a 'hold ya' (hold here or hold this) boy, to hold tools and hand them to the workman.

In some instances, of course, the boy can be learning a skill:

> When I am not in school I usually went to a Cabinet shop near my home where I learn my trade. In the shop I help the men to finish up their work. Sometime People ask me to make picture for them and I am glad to do the job. The men in the shop show me how to control the machine in the shop and Shows me How made things in Carpentery. So that why I am quite Capable of being a Carpenter when I am much older. (15-year-old, Kingston).

In an unstructured situation in a small enterprise, the degree of exploitation as well as the degree of skill acquisition depend very largely upon the ability and nature of individual employers.

The boys tend to begin this type of work by hanging around a workshop where the work and workmen appear congenial.

> When I am not in school I usually visit a welding shop to watch how the employers (employees) are doing there job . . . As times go by and me and those employers became friends when they had their spare time they would show me how to weld as well as tell me some of the name of the parts that are in the engin. (15-year-old urban boy).

Work with cars is particularly favoured. As soon as a boy can be useful, usually at about 13, he may be put to work.

> On Wednesdays when I am not at school I went to the workshop and help the man on the buses, the cars and on the van, sometime (could mean 'once'). I take it to my mother and she say that I must keep it for myself. (14-year-old, Kingston)

The principal of one Kingston school stated that these apprenticeships are very unstructured relationships and are usually between a boy and the owner of a small workshop. The student 'might be paid or he might not be paid'. Often a parent makes the arrangement for the boy 'as a sort of understanding' and they often seem to feel that this is better than attending school, especially for slow learners.

Sometimes the financial circumstances of the household torce the

29

child to leave school and enter employment. Thus the parent, by finding some kind of skill training, is taking the best available action for the child's future. On other occasions, the child may be encouraged to substitute for a parent in order to keep a scarce job within the household. In this way children are encouraged into employment as part of the overall household survival strategy.

> When I am not in school, I go to the University Hospital of the West Indies and learn engineer work. I work as a service man, like if my father or next workman dont come I work in his space. Example, fix tyre fix motor car or anytime get an emergency call I look after it.
> If my father goes on sick leaf (leave) I has to work for him until he come back to work.
> (Grade 10, Kingston).

It is not only boys who are involved in these situations but, as female unemployment in the 14 to 24 age group is double that of male, the opportunities for apprenticeships are correspondingly lower for girls. Where apprentice work is available, family links are almost inevitably involved.

> My mother send me to my aunt to learn to sew clothes. I would sit and sew for whole day. Sometimes I make hankerchiefs, socks and stocking. My aunt took them to the market and sole (sold) them for me.
> (13-year-old rural girl).

It was reported to us that children also substitute for the parents in this way in the 'Crash Programme' which is a government jobs creation project in which the work performed is usually street cleaning or cutting grass verges. Some of the children in our sample did mention this. We were told that children substitute for, or work alongside, parents in plantations, particularly where payment is at piece rate. In some monoculture areas the soil is in any case unsuitable for anything other than the main crop. Thus little or no family labour farming is possible to supplement either diet or income. Children help their parents during the long sugar harvest. Because this is piece work, they are useful to get the tasks done. A teacher stated 'It doesn't matter to parents what age they are', but the most usual age to begin is 12 years old and they may continue to be absent from school for two or three months in the season.

Although most of the children working regularly in Jamaica do part-time, seasonal or holiday jobs there is still some cause for concern. Some children obviously work long hours over and above their time at school. If such a child is malnourished, as many are, their health can suffer. Several children complained of tiredness caused by working and stated that they were unable to complete school assignments because of this. In addition, many children begin to do part-time work which fits in with the school shift system. But shifts are alternated either by the term or annually. School principals mentioned that, when this happened, the child usually gave up school rather than his employment. A possible solution to this problem, if the child clearly needed the income, or wanted to keep doing a job which could prevent him or her being unemployed as a school leaver, might be to allow such children to continue on the convenient shift when shifts were changed. There are guidance counsellors in secondary schools who could be available to organise these matters. But, in our experience, guidance counsellors were almost wholly concerned with sex and family life education and seldom dealt with economic problems. Moreover, because of its authoritarian nature, the Jamaican education system is inflexible and does not face up to the realities of the situation.

Fishing

Fishing represents a particular form of apprenticeship within the regular economy and recruitment is related to family life. Despite the fact that fish is traditionally a major source of protein for Jamaicans, the fishing industry contributes only about 0.7 per cent of the annual gross domestic product. Large quantities of dried fish have always been imported, until recent problems with foreign exchange caused shortages in this, as in so many other essential items. The importance of fish protein in the diet was illustrated by the number of teachers in fishing areas who commented upon the better standard of nutrition among children from fishing families.

The domestic fishing industry catches around 18,000 tons of fish a year and employs about 7,000 people, either wholly or partially. The industry operates on a small scale. Fishing takes place largely inshore, in open canoes carrying up to four people. In recent years a government-financed scheme to provide engines has resulted in fishing taking place further from shore. We received several reports of children leaving school to be 'apprenticed' to fishermen, who were not infrequently kinsmen. Undoubtedly, these boys would be attracted by the high incomes available to fishermen, who can earn up to 200 dollars with a good catch. This makes them appear better off than cane-cutters earning 30 to 40 dollars a day on piece work. Precisely because fishing is an uncertain mode of earning a living, a good day tends to be treated as a windfall and fishermen do not always spend wisely. In Jamaican fishing villages, as in many fishing communities elsewhere, there are free-spenders, men who appear to be always in the money. This probably accounts for much of the attraction of fishing among adolescent boys. It seems far more exciting than acquiring the seemingly irrelevant skills of numeracy and literacy which the apparently wealthy fisherman probably lacks.

31

In a nuclear family, fathers do the fishing, while mothers sell the catch. But many children live in female-headed households and these children become involved in marketing activities. Because the industry is so small in scale there are no cold storage facilities and thus the large number of vendors is responsible for distribution from the beaches. Children are involved in all three operations of catching, distribution and sale, either with parents or on their own account. Boys from single parent families, who are unable to fish with their fathers, are reported to 'cut' (steal) fish from the beaches to sell.

It was reported to us that some boys go to sea part-time as early as grade 7 (age 12 to 13 years). As fishing operations take place between dusk and dawn and the catch has to be sold on the beach, they are often exhausted when they arrive at school and may fall asleep during lessons. Those who have no fathers may have to catch fish throughout the night and then help their mothers to pack up the load and catch a bus to Kingston to sell in the market. One principal stated 'these are the ones who eventually drop out, because they have been so conditioned to the adult way of life'. The work is arduous and if it forms part of a family enterprise, the youth may not receive much financial remuneration.

During the school days and I am on afternoon shift, I have to wake up five
o'clock to go to sea with my grandfather.
The works that I have to perform out there . . . are very hard. I have to
paddle the boat, help to draw the fish pots. Sometimes when I left my home at
five o'clock in the morning I usually come back to about eleven o'clock . . .
and from there I have to leave for school.
During the weekends and the holidays I still have a lot of works to do. I still
have to go to sea, sometimes when we catch a lot of fish, I may get a two pound
for myself so that I can sell to earn a living.
(17-year-old, north coast).

But the lure of high incomes still attracts recruits and feeds unrealistic
ambitions. As one boy wrote, 'When I go to sea and come back I sel the
Fish and the money I get I use it to buy Race Horse' (16-year-old, south
coast).

It is clear that, if they actually gain a place on a boat, these boys are
not just joy-riding passengers. They perform a difficult and dangerous job
of work and learn some skills.

I go to sea with my father's boat . . . Before I go to sea I put the net into the
boat about 3 am three have (of) us then we go for the engain (engine). We put
it on the boat, we bull (pour?) it into the boat. We put the Ice box into the boat
with about one hundred ice, then we leave. We take about I hour to reach
were (where) we going to. The We shout (shoot) out the net into the sea. We
leave the net into the (sea) for about one hour then we take it up back and we
cought about five waight (cwt?) of fish one waight of paratfish, one waight
of grunt fish, two waight of Jack fish one waight of snapper fish. We cought
some Welchman fish too. Then we make a nix (the next) set. We wait tell (till)
day lite out and sun come up about 8:0'clock We set and we ice up the fish, and
make five more set and come back to shure (shore) about 2 o'clock.
(16-year-old, south coast).

The Informal sector

Household labour

As stated above some boys from fishing families join a family enterprise
and begin to fish around the age of 13. The number of childen engaged in
this is relatively small according to our sample and this reflects the small
size of the fishing industry. A far more common source of labour, as in so
much of the developing world, is on family farms but evidence about the
extent of child involvement is conflicting. Judging from our data, most
children, even in the metropolitan areas, perform some agricultural task.
Often this only amounts to feeding and watering the goats or chickens
which wander even on busy thoroughfares. These are daily chores which
have to be completed before or after school. Most rural children also

mentioned helping adults with crops in the fields and many stated that they had their own 'field' which probably amounted to little more than a small plot.

We recorded such agricultural tasks as labour only if the jobs written about appeared arduous or if they prevented children from going to school. But agriculture as a household enterprise may affect children in ways other than by using their labour on the land. For instance, a child may be required to perform tasks within the house in order to free adults for the more physically demanding work in the fields. Moreover, children in rural areas are often kept home to help prepare a load for market.

Prior to the Second World War, Jamaica was a predominantly agricultural country, but during the past two decades due to both internal and external migration, there has been a sharp decrease in the agricultural population. Although large plantations account for over half the available acreage, there is a numerical predominance of multiproduct, small-acreage farms. Bananas are a particularly important crop because they provide a reliable source of income, require little capital outlay, yield regularly and harvest throughout the year. Together with sugar, bananas are Jamaica's main export crops. Some 60 per cent of the banana crop is produced on smallholdings.

But farming is not a favoured occupation. Only 1 per cent of children in our study gave agricultural pursuits as a career preference. Most small-scale farms do not provide adequate income for self-sufficiency. Farm households tend to rely on wage labour or other income from outside activities; men may follow a trade, while women are usually involved in marketing.

In 1968, 77.96 per cent of all farms were smaller than five acres and fragmentation of the smaller farms is on the increase (O Jefferson, *The Post-war Economic Development of Jamaica*, ISER 1972). This is largely brought about by the land tenure and inheritance practices. Yields are low and because of a combination of the small size of the average farm and of the generally hilly terrain, there is little mechanisation. The insecurity of land tenure, which is often on annual leases, inhibits farmers from making significant improvements or even from planting semi-permament crops. The systems of inheritance and joint ownership, frequently mean that no member of the family will cultivate the land for fear that a relation will claim a share of the crop. Often the actual farmer is a woman on her own and farming provides the only income with which she can buy food for her dependent children. Because of the time spent caring for her offspring, she will not have the time, energy or expertise to improve the land or even make best use of it.

A 13-year-old suburban girl in our sample stated that such cash crops as lettuce and tomatoes, because of their short growing seasons, were cultivated on her small farm, adding 'mother does this farming for a living so I am often stop from school to help her'. This pattern of small scale, multicrop farming is very common. A 15-year-old boy drew for us a picture of his father's farm, on which the main crops were yams, sugar cane, red and green peas and bananas.

The only relatively large-scale farming which was mentioned by any of the children in our sample was the illegal crop ganja (marijuana), which is grown in large quantities in hilly areas in the north of the island, and can attract many children away from school because of the large profits it can provide. As one 14-year-old in this area wrote, (in an essay decorated with accurate drawings of cannabis plants), his preferred career was 'to be a ganja seller',

> When I am not at school I go to the feal (field) with father to help him in the fiel plant ganga to get the sail beacouse ganga is selling now one pond (pound) of ganga is selling for $30.

The marketing system reflects the small scale of agricultural enterprises. As in the case of fishing, the distribution of goods is performed by a countrywide network of small-scale merchants, usually women, known as higglers. They are characterised by the small quantities

35

of products in whch they deal, for they have no storage facilities. A diversity of produce, often governed by seasonal availability, is their stock in trade and they form a nationwide marketing system, via public transport, private mini-buses and truckers with whom they may hitch lifts. Despite the small scale of their operations, it has been characteristic of higglers since the eighteenth century that they use money as a medium of exchange and do not barter. The relationship between the higgler system and child labour will be further discussed in the section on street labour.

In this section we are less concerned with the generation of actual cash income, through activities outside the household, than with the child's contribution to the domestic economy through activities which cannot be described as occupations. Commercial family enterprises such as shops, bars or dressmaking establishments accounted for some of the household labour of the children in our sample. But childen in non-productive work at home can free adults for productive labour in a family enterprise or in one outside. This category of employment accounted for the highest percentage of child labour in our sample, despite the fact that we ignored many examples of domestic work when making our content analysis. We even discounted some cases in which a child complained about the amount of housework he or she was expected to do. Few childen in any society fail to grumble about the tasks which parents ask them to perform in the home.

In addition, it is necessary to remember that 'childhood' does not have the same meaning in all cultures. The idea of childhood as a time of innocence, a period in which individuals are in need of particular kinds of protection has developed in Western nations over the past 200 years, as Phillipe Aries showed in his book *Centuries of Childhood* (Penguin 1979). Twentieth-century educational psychology has encouraged the notion of childhood as an extended period of play, learning and personality development, during which adult responsibilities and attitudes are absent. But in Jamaica, as in many other parts of the developing world, young people are regarded as responsible members of an economic unit, with responsibilities to other members from an early age. Children quickly become accustomed to an order of priorities. First, they are responsible to, and for, other people in the household and must perform certain domestic tasks. Second, they have responsibilities for performing school work. Third and last, come the individual's commitment to play, personal leisure and hobbies – an area which is usually regarded as a natural function of childhood in the West. This order of priorities was, almost without exception, reflected in the essays collected. The following is a fairly typical summary of the day of a 14-year-old girl.

36

some of the things I would do are cleaning the house. washing the dishes also dirty clothes, give my baby sister a bath fetch water tidy the outsides of the house the kitchen and keep the place clean and tidy. After finishing that work I would study lessons . . . (then) I would help my brother and sister with their work.

In the twelve o'clock and I would given them thier lunch and started off for the farm to collect food for the family then I would go and look for the animal to give them water and to look if they are okay then I would (go) to the shop to collect something for dinner boil our dinner eat it play Baseball have a bath and go to our bed.

The order of priorities even appears in the drawings on the following pages made by younger children.

Both boys and girls are involved in household and agricultural tasks. Many boys reported washing and ironing clothes and caring for younger children and girls frequently wrote of going to the fields to work. Most children have daily chores from the time they can walk. The concept of childhood as a time of play and period of no responsibilities is not current among the poor majority in Jamaica. It can be difficult to argue a case of direct exploitation, if household and agricultural work by children is part of those learning and socialisation processes which tend to take place within families. It may be necessary for all available labour to be used to ensure that subsistence needs are met on a small peasant holding, particularly on labour-intensive work such as harvesting and on non-mechanised farms. The essays also suggest that some parents stop children from attending school and require them to perform household tasks which the children considered as not absolutely necessary, or to do work which could be physically harmful.

Training in household tasks to the exclusion of play or education begins early in Jamaica. One basic school (pre-school) teacher said that her charges did not really know how to play. For some children, even for those younger than five, daily life consists of a sequence of chores. When urged to play, they simply mime the household tasks which they are obviously used to performing. This teacher insisted that the children are not playfully imitating adult life, but reflecting their own existence: 'they are little drudges'.

In an attempt to test this statement, we asked 98 children in the five to eight age range and all attending the same rural all-age school, to draw pictures or write essays on the topic we had given the older children. We then aggregated the number of times a particular activity was either mentioned or drawn; this can be seen in the table on page 40.
The range of activities speaks for itself. Play is ranked only sixth in the list and other tasks appear, such as carrying water or chopping wood, which are heavy for a small child. We were also disturbed by the number of children under eight years old who are involved in child care, because it is

I am carring water

I am going to sweep yard

I am staying with a baby

I am feeding the dog

I am going
to fieldo

I am stay
whit papa

I am going to
look for frend

I am going to climb the tree
to pick breadgiurt

Sweeping the yard   32
Cleaning house/washing clothes   31
Carrying water   29
Going on errands or shopping   23
Working in the field   20
Playing   20
Caring for animals (could be pets)   15
Catching food (e.g. fishing)   12
Child care   12
Chopping wood   9
Reading a book   7

clear that in some cases they are left alone with this responsibility. Many of the drawings amply illustrate the scale of tasks for a small child. In a picture of child care the baby sits on a huge chair which dominates the picture and dwarfs the older child. The tap of a standpipe from which water is to be carried towers above the child's head. The broom to sweep the yard is longer by far than the child who wields it and a pan for cooking or washing is big enough for it to sit in.

The degree of responsibility which this early emphasis produces is clear in many essays:

When I have work to do I just have to do it, so it doesn't make sense when I am talking about feeling lazy because I just have to do it and dont say anything. (15-year-old girl).

When I am home I work hard like as to mother. My mother of (have) to go to town about four or three days in the week so I of to do here (her) work. (16-year-old girl).

The skills and self-confidence to shoulder adult responsibility adequately are acquired early, as this 11-year-old primary schoolchild, left in charge of a baby, younger children, a shop and a home, illustrates:

It was on a Friday when I was absent from school, because my mother wasn't going to be at home, and I had to stay home.
On that particular day, I had to stay with my little baby sister which is approximately two months, above all things I had to tidy the house, and give an eye on the shop, because I was the only person at home, except for my smaller brother and sister. They too help me by staying out front and telling me when someone needs to be served. When I'm not in the shop, I'm in the house tiding or nursing the baby.
After I had finished tiding the house I had another problem, and the problem was the baby. Although I have given her her bath and had fed her she didn't want to sleep so I locked the shop and took her up and sang her a 'rock a by' song until she finally went to bed and my problem was solved. Then I opened the shop and as I opened the shop my mother had arrived. She was very tired when she came, and I still had to stay in the shop while she went inside and rested awhile. Soon it was nightfall and I went to bed early because I was going out the next morning.

While some children stay at home willingly to perform these duties, considerable pressure is exerted on others to make them miss the schooling they feel they need. 'My mother have a spite on me' wrote one student, while another complained that she could not make her mother understand that she should go to school every day. An older girl reported that her schooling was affected 'To be frank, when I get home in the days I always have house work to do, and if I dont do it there will be some sort of quarrelling. When I am through with washing of dishes and ironing I feel tired sometimes, and then I do no schoolwork.'

Tiredness is a frequent complaint.

After weeding, there is no need for me to say I am going to rest because mother is very hard and love to work.
I was so busy doing every little thing I can manage. When I was half the way to finish I was so tired. I sat down and while I was sitting there I fell asleep. While I was there I felt someone hit me on my back. I jump up and look around, I was so frightened it was my mother. When I saw that it was my mother I started to cry. She hit me again and said go and finish what I had to do.

In Edith Clark's book, *My Mother who Fathered Me*, to which we referred earlier, the Jamaican mother is described as a dependable noble matriarch. But in the above essay, a mother appears in the more realistic guise of an exhausted and irritated single parent, angry with a life which forces her out to work, faced with far too much work to do, with a heavy burden of responsibility, and coping at the same time with feelings of guilt about keeping a child at home to perform household tasks which are beyond its skills or energies. Although Jamaican society is predominantly matrifocal there is a tendency for people to act as if the nuclear family is the norm. Single mothers are caught in this contradictory set of values. They have the economic capacity to be self-sufficient but they are psychologically dependent upon men for support; on having a man and producing babies to 'keep him'. Although most women, in fact, cope on their own (and cope extremely well for all or part of their adult lives) they are still made to feel failures for being in a situation in which they have to be autonomous.

When the mother has to be the father, it is inevitable that in many cases children have to be housewives, dealing with the frustrations and boredoms of a role which has been thrust upon them, rather than being brought about by their own actions. As one 17-year-old girl wrote:

> When I am not in school, I have to stay with my mother's baby Because mother have to go to work and she ask me to stay with the baby for her and until she gets somebody to stay with her and then we can get to go to school. If she cannot get anybody we can not go to school, because she is working and she have rent to pay clothes to buy, and foods to buy. Staying at home come boring to me and in the house is very dark at day when me a lonly in the house some times . . . and my (baby) sister is so miserable and hot, and I ca not do eanything about it . . .

If the mothers had regular jobs, it would be possible to make out a case for free or subsidised creche facilities at the workplace. But most women are employed as domestic servants or are self-employed higglers. Day nurseries and pre-school education are expensive items for which the Jamaican state cannot reasonably be expected to increase provision. The Maternity Leave Act No 44, 1979 provides for paid maternity leave. Although this is an important advance in principle, in practice it will really affect only the middle-class minority, for it applies only to regular wage earners. At one school in our study, the principal had tried encouraging children to bring their younger siblings to an informal creche at school. She reported that this temporary and experimental scheme had substantially improved attendance figures while it was in operation. It is an idea which could and should be explored by educational authorities. But this is unlikely so long as they adhere to an outdated and inappropriate authoritarian ideal of education instead of espousing creativity and flexibility.

It is unusual for Jamaican children to suffer wilful neglect. But, although children are welcomed and valued by mothers, this is not necessarily for sentimental reasons. They are valued as economic assets and regarded as an insurance against poverty in old age. The shifting nature of the child population has already been mentioned. This is often related to the fact that children live in a variety of alternative households as well as in matrifocal and nuclear families. Of the 1,097 children in our sample who gave an indication of their household composition, only 22 per cent were clearly living in a nuclear family. Eighty-one children were living in female-headed homes (mother, grandmother or aunt) while a further 668 children mentioned only a mother and were therefore likely to be living in a matrifocal household. The total percentage of probable matrifocal homes in our sample was therefore well over 50 per cent (Figure 9). But children living with a father alone, with other relatives, with guardians and even completely alone also occurred in our sample.

Those cases of children who live with a non-parental relative or with a guardian or foster parent, illustrate both the common occurrence of fostering in Jamaica and the way in which the domestic labour of children is valued in the strategies of survival. It is accepted that adults who do not have a child in the household will seek to obtain their labour. Thus a grade 8 suburban girl wrote that 'I have to go down to my aunt to help her to do some work because she is very sickly she lives by herself I clean for her on Friday', and an 11-year-old stated that she often visited her grandfather

> when he is sick and cannot go to work. I would tidy up the house. When I'm finished I would go to the shop and buy everything, coconut, green bananas, sugar, flour, and rice and place them in the cupboard . . . After that I would carry the water and put it in the jar.

An older girl wrote that she and her three younger siblings were living with a cousin rather than with parents and 'That mean I have more work to do'. And although an only daughter quoted her mother frequently saying that 'a house without a child is no home at all' this did not prevent her being sent to stay with a widowed and dying grandmother.

In discussions with child welfare officials, it was suggested to us that a wide variety of unofficial fostering strategies probably accounts for an unknown amount of domestic labour and possible exploitation. Rural children with good educational potential may be sent in to towns to live with a relative or acquaintance so that they can benefit from the relatively better educational opportunities. Alternatively, particularly in recent years, urban children are sent to rural areas because of the apparently greater availability of food. In either case, the household to which the child is sent may be virtually unknown to the parent. The transaction may

43

Sweeping the House

take place in the market through the medium of one of the peripatetic higglers.

The child is usually expected to provide domestic labour in return for its keep. Promises that the urban foster household will ensure that the child goes to school or training college may be given but never realised. A member of the Child Welfare Department claimed that this process was also experienced 'in a subtle way' with official fostering arrangements. Thus an elderly, middle-class woman with grown up children would ask to foster a 14 or 15-year-old girl 'to keep me company'. But the department would be suspicious of motives in such cases. They stated that fostering arrangements usually begin well, with the child being provided with a pleasant room and being treated as one of the family. In many cases, however, conditions deteriorate within a week or so. Then the child 'lives in a back room', eats separately from the family and has to do domestic work. According to the department, this can lead to a girl being morally at risk. She is 'enslaved' into the system until a boy 'pays court' and persuades her to go and live with him. During our research, we found one case of a 14-year-old orphan living with an elderly woman. She had become pregnant by her guardian's 40-year-old son.

The final comment we should like to make about domestic labour concerns the structure of family life. Teenage pregnancy is regarded, by state and international agencies, as a severe Jamaican problem. It is a major cause of dropping out among teenage girls and is probably exacerbated by the very high rate of unemployment among girls in the 15 to 24 age group. There are some opportunities available for girls of high academic ability, but adolescent girls who have not achieved academic success can perceive no career opportunities and fall back all too readily upon child bearing. In this they are encouraged by the high value placed upon motherhood and the equally high value placed upon the acquisition of children by a household. The ideal is to be supported by a male breadwinner and it was reported to us throughout the island that it is often the brightest girls in secondary schools who get pregnant first. This possibly reflects a semi-deliberate choice of career (as child bearer), because it is equally widely-reported that the father in a teenage pregnancy is usually in his middle or late twenties. In other words he is not a schoolboy, but an adult who could provide maintenance particularly if he is in regular employment. Indeed it was reported to us at one school that mothers encourage their teenage daughters to take a lover who can visit at weekends and bring luxuries which can be shared with other members of the household. This claim was not directly substantiated by any case material, but our evidence does indicate that in many families this situation would not be discouraged by the mother.

Street vending
We have grouped under this heading various modes of acquiring a cash income from casual labour in Jamaica's streets and market places. Although our sample does not reveal a substantial proportion of children engaged in street labour, this is a function of the nature of the sample itself. As we shall show, this type of labour is most frequently engaged in by those children who never enrolled in school or who have dropped out. Although we have examples of street labour from the essays, most of the evidence in this section comes from our observations of children working in and around the Kingston area and particularly from interviews with a group of eight to 15-year-old street corner hustlers.

The recognised form of street labour in Jamaica is selling, which may, in fact, appear in official statistics because it is a widespread phenomenon and has a long history. The higgling network has already been mentioned.

But this internal marketing system only accounts for the movement of locally grown produce from rural areas into urban markets. Also operating in the street are two other types of merchants, which we designate the urban vendor and the import vendor. The stock in trade of the urban vendor is small quantities of locally manufactured goods, locally acquired goods and goods purchased from higglers. The import vendor is a new style of higgler, who deals in 'foreign' goods which have been purchased abroad, either in other Caribbean islands or in Miami. Onions from the Cayman Islands and shoes from Miami were two major vendor imports at the time of fieldwork and during March, when local cigarette factories were on strike, the only source of cigarettes on the island were street vendors.

A child's insertion into this marketing complex may be simple and may operate only at the family or household level. It may not bring the child any direct income, but merely entail that some time is spent helping a higgler mother, particularly in rural areas, collect and pack a load for market. The content of these loads varies. It may consist of seasonal produce from a smallholding or as we have already seen, it may be the produce of a fishing enterprise. But very small quantities of fruit in season are often gathered from the bush:

> When I am away from school I carry bananas for my mother and pack them up that he (she) can get them to carry to market on thursday. It is not only banana I have to pack. I pack coconut and plantains.
> (Grade 9 urban girl

> Theur days (Thursdays) I go to the bush with my mother to look load for Friday market.
> (Grade 8 suburban boy)

> When mongo (mango) comes in I go to pick mongo with my sister to sell at the market.
> (Grade 8 suburban girl)

Occasionally the market place is not in the town, but simply by the roadside in rural areas. Along most main roads through the countryside there are scattered groups of stalls. Children are frequently in charge of these and they stay at the roadside all day, often waving their rural products at passing cars. And of course there are local markets for local produce:

> Sometime I go to the river and shoot fish and sold them to my nabour (neighbour) who is nair by, then when I sold them I give my mother the money then she would give me some money to go to school the next day and I would tell the teacher the reason why I could not come to school . . .
> (14-year-old boy in urban tourist area).

It is characteristic for a child to assume responsibility for its own upkeep. As pointed out earlier, it is part of the role learnt in early childhood. In the island-wide pattern of higglering, children quickly learn the tricks needed for successful hawking and peddling. Jamaica in 1980 is a real subsistence economy where what is at stake is survival. The marketing complex thus has priority over the more esoteric advantages of literacy and numeracy. Even when children are given their own small plot of land it is not in order to exploit their labour, or even to teach them farming skills, but rather to accustom them to the marketing mentality.

In addition to farming, children become familiar with a large range of small scale manufacturing activities which fill a local market need. The range of activities is bewilderingly large:

> Sometimes I had to help my Grandmother Beet is chocolate (cook her chocolate) to sell to make a living.
> Some of the day when I finish work I go and help my uncle with some of is (his) bees box frame . . . Some Times I go and (get?) honey and when I finish strain it get some . . . bottle and full them with honey and they are Ready to sell.
> (17-year-old urban boy).

> I go to the market with my aunt and help her sell syrup, pudding, matches and other things.
> (16-year-old metropolitan girl living with her aunt and a brother).

A 12-year-old rural murder victim was described in one newspaper report as an 'active' boy, who made and sold drops (coconut sweets). He used the money to 'buy drop pan' (take part in a Chinese gambling game) on which he had won money intended for the purchase of a bicycle. (*Sunday Sun*, Kingston, 10 February 1980, p3).

An urban schoolteacher described one form of manufacture which seemed to be particularly common at the time of fieldwork. The need for the product was obvious; paper bags were in very short supply and all supermarkets carried notices that many goods could not be wrapped. On Thursdays and Fridays particularly, the chidren from this teacher's primary school stayed at home, to make paper bags, either alone or with other household members. Waste, such as old cement or animal feed bags, was made into smaller bags and sold to vendors in the market place. Other children went to a local factory which makes plastic bags. They utilised excess plastic or sometimes bought ready-made bags which they filled with scallion (rather like spring onion), thyme and other cheap produce which could be collected or purchased. These pre-packaged goods were then sold in the market place. It was an interesting characteristic that several household members might be engaged in selling operations at the one time; so that the entire marketing area could be covered and household labour maximised. A parent or other adult would be the base and the children would walk around the market place, selling small quantities of the household stock. Or a mother might sit at a stall on one side of the road, while her children sold at separate points on the other side; one with plastic bags, one with paper bags, and another with oranges or other farm produce.

> I go out and help my mother to sell in the market meanwhile she is buying some thing to sell in the market I am helping here (her) selling. (14-year-old rural child).

In the range of goods mentioned by children, or observed by us, were sweets, ice lollies, biscuits, 'foreign thing' (imported goods), earthenware pots and cooked food, but there are clearly many others. Ganja is sold by some but it is in plentiful supply on the island and, except in tourist areas, does not provide a particularly lucrative source of income. Large incomes are gained by adults in illegal export, but 'selling the weed' to tourists is only one of a set of tourist-associated services, like 'taking them for walks' (sightseeing) or acting as ball boys in tennis games. Tourism also encourages begging. But there are other 'occupations' which offer a better income in tourist regions, as opposed to other urban areas, such as taking empty soft-drink bottles from tables outside cafes and hotels to obtain the deposit money.

Selling does not always take place in the market itself. Children will enter offices, banks and post offices in order to peddle their wares and often hang around tourist spots looking for customers. Small towns have regular market places but, in the metropolitan area in particular, the selling arena is the pavement, which is often so thronged with vendors that it is difficult to move. Other favourite areas are plazas, the shopping complexes which have grown up since the late 1960s.

Children, particularly boys in the 10 to 15 age range, often set up in business on their own, using carts which they push or cycle into residential areas. Peanut vending is particularly popular, and the peanuts are toasted on the carts. Typical among these were two boys (aged about 13 and 16) who pushed a heavy wooden cart around the hot, uneven streets of Kingston. They worked seven days a week from early morning until late at night. The roaster was equipped with a shrill and deafening steam whistle, through which they heralded their arrival. We interviewed another group of three boys (all under 14) well after midnight, as they sold hot, roasted peanuts outside a dance hall. As it was carnival time (celebrated by Trinidadian residents of Jamaica) they expected to make about 30 dollars that night by selling peanuts at 50 cents a bag. The 11-year-old, who owned the cart, stated that he went out selling every day and that his usual earnings were around 2 dollars a day, but we suspected that this might be higher.

Such enterprise is not the norm however. Other children turn their hands to a variety of hustling methods of earning a living on the street.

Begging is one mode, as are bottle collecting, carrying goods from supermarkets to cars and so forth.

Particular parts of the metropolitan area are associated with hustling. An extensive study, made by a geographer of Kingston in the 1960s, identified what the author called 'slums of despair', where there was little hope of ever finding regular wage employment. One means of scratching a living was 'living on the dungle' or combing through rubbish tips to find saleable goods and materials which had been discarded by the more prosperous citizens. (C G Clarke, *Kingston, Jamaica: Urban Growth and Social Change*, Berkeley 1975). The more notorious of the 'dungle' areas have been cleared since Clarke wrote his book but the stark poverty and need remain. Such modes of generating an income still exist. Children in these situations cannot be adequately dealt with by police and social workers. The police are empowered, as one social worker stated, to 'scrape them off the streets' but, because of a lack of residential facilities, those who need custodial care are denied it. Those who are placed in care often abscond because they are not used to discipline. The police are frustrated by the situation and, in any case, these children present a relatively minor problem compared with the high rate of violent adult crime on the island.

The adult responsibility thrust upon children can easily become associated with delinquency. A school principal in a metropolitan slum area said that children with migrant or from 'single mother' families experience severe social problems. Many of these children are left alone while mothers work or others live with friends or by themselves. They are early forced to fend for themselves and to become self-sufficient. It is impossible for school authorities to enforce discipline. When children are told to bring a parent to school to discuss poor behaviour, they will reply 'There's nobody I have to bring'. Many parents also find discipline difficult. Children who have to perform adult tasks at home may consequently require to be treated as adults. They do not take easily to discipline; they rebel. Some leave home altogether, and they may do this if their parents demand too great a portion of the day's hustling earnings. In the early evenings, child street hustlers can often be seen eating huge 'take away' meals before going home to hand over the remainder of their earnings. The child has to sell or hustle to survive. The importance of immediate cash income or return becomes an early and stultifying influence upon the child's view of himself and his life. They may start with higgling or vending but, if the rewards are too small, they may turn to gambling and to stealing, both of which provide, at least potentially, bigger and quicker returns for labour input. Juvenile offenders who come before the family court are mostly boys. Mothers tend to keep girls at home and teenage girls may well have babies to look after.

49

In our sample, there were three schoolchildren living alone and, as we have seen, this is not uncommon, particularly in the metropolitan area. These children are less likely to go to school and more likely to be drawn into criminal activities out of need. Several of the child street workers we knew in Kingston admitted to living rough in parks from time to time. Children living outside society in this way quickly learn how to support themselves by illegal means.

If children are involved in criminal activities later readjustment is difficult and can even prove impossible. A drop-out or temporary absentee may have his or her capacity to benefit from the disciplined atmosphere of school still further eroded within a very short time.

As we have seen, many children obviously see crime as the only viable alternative mode of existence if they are unable to obtain a job after finishing school. Others are acutely aware of the very thin defence of household resources which separates them from starvation. Many referred to the need to 'ful my belly'. Stated ambitions in essays were frequently as simple as a job and a house to live in. When a group of street boys were asked what their major ambition would be if any wish could be granted, the typical response was food, a house, a wife and, for only one boy, a car. But most could not even visualise these possibilities and wished only for a suit and shoes. These were boys, of between eight and fifteen, who had already dropped out of school. For them, street hustling had become a way of life to which they could see no end, and their chances of ever managing to return to school, of becoming literate, and of having even the chance to become serious applicants for regular jobs, were remote.

Juvenile delinquency

Jamaican children of all classes are aware of the particularly high rate of violent crime on the island. This is reflected in one of the interviews we recorded. A street boy stated that his father was dead and another boy chimed in with the question 'Who killed him?' It is easy for children to become involved in violence. The extent of youth crime may be judged by the fact that in 1978, 64 per cent of convictions for major crimes were received by people under 25. Many of these convictions were for crimes of violence. During the particularly violent General Election of 1972 and again in 1976, gun battles were fought between followers of the two major political parties, the Peoples National Party (PNP) and the Jamaica Labour Party (JLP). In 1975 the PNP government of Michael Manley passed what has become known as the 'Gun Law'. This makes a life sentence mandatory for all those convicted of gun crimes.

The South Camp Rehabilitation Centre was set up in the heart of Kingston to serve as a place of detention for all those convicted in the Special Gun Court where proceedings are heard in camera. In 1978, 56 per cent of those admitted to the South Camp Rehabilitation Centre were under 25. The average age of those convicted in the Gun Court has remained under 20 throughout its operation (Department of Correctional Services (Jamaica) Annual Report 1978). At the time of fieldwork, there was reason to believe that juveniles under the age of 16 were being held in the South Camp Rehabilitation Centre.

Major crimes account for about half of the offences committed every year in Jamaica. Some areas of West Kingston are associated with violent crimes and gunmen.

As 1980 was an election year, much of this violence was described as political. Particular areas of the town are strongholds for the supporters of one or other of the two major political parties. It was impossible to live in safety in these areas without supporting the appropriate party. Children were rapidly involved in these party allegiances. The borders of the territories are so well defined, the personnel so well known to each other, that children are unable to cross a rival territory to go to school. But the violent rivalry, often referred to locally as 'tribalism', does not depend entirely upon devotion to party political ideology. The Jamaican political system is based on patron-client relations. This is frequently the case when there are insufficient resources and control over them is in the hands of a powerful minority. As the leader of the Jamaica Workers Party has written (T Monroe, *The Politics of Constitutional Decolonisation*, ISER Jamaica 1972, p.199), deprivation among the urban poor, particularly the unemployed, 'makes them available for use as political gangsters in return for handouts or promises of one kind or another'.

One adolescent boy told us he did not finish school:

'because some de guys over dere know me an say is round dat wey ah comin. I come from (Kingston suburb) say dem goin t'mash mi down yuh no see it. So I didn' wan get no 'wit so ah stop go over dere'.

Because so many of the scarce employment opportunities are in the public sector, it is relatively easy for patronage to develop, particularly in those jobs where labour is paid on a weekly or casual basis. It is not only jobs which can be supplied in return for political support, but also more basic items like food and housing. Violence helps to maintain territories and spheres of influence within the urban ghetto. According to first-hand information, youths are formed into gangs which ensure that the territory is not attacked, and they police the area to ward off intruders. Usually the boys begin these activities at 15 or 16 years of age. But we came across the case of an 11-year-old who carried a gun, and all the street boys we met, carried knives or other sharp weapons as a matter of course. A school principal ventured to suggest that cash payments of about five to 10 dollars a week might be paid for the services of these teenage gunmen. but it is also likely that their support would be paid for in kind.

Violence is also manifest in other major crimes. Weapons are freely available. About one fifth of juveniles (legally those under 17) who are sent to approved schools are convicted of violent crimes against the person. Few of the remainder are convicted of minor offences, and most of the juveniles admitted to approved schools have been involved in offences against property. In 1978, 66 children under 14 were admitted to approved school. Only 11 were there under care and protection orders. and only five had been found guilty of minor crimes. Of the rest. 34 were under restraint for larceny and associated offences and 16 for crimes such as assault and wounding. It is likely that these figures only hint at the extent to which children are involved in various kinds of stealing.

Another possible source of income, in the illegal sector of casual employment, is prostitution. We inquired into this, but could find no direct evidence that it took place among juveniles. But this may not be the case. as is indicated in a letter which appeared in the Kingston newspaper the *Sunday Sun* on 10 February 1980. The writer claimed that before her religious conversion at the age of 17 she had been living as a prostitute and thief. smoking ganja and drinking heavily. She also stated that she had to seek treatment for venereal disease. Novels apparently set in the early 1970s also refer to teenage prostitution. for instance *Children of Sysiphus* by Jamaican author Orlando Patterson (Kingston 1974). Our impression is that. although organised prostitution is not a major part of Jamaican criminal activities. many girls are exploited sexually. Although this may bring them some form of maintenance. they do not receive recompense in cash or even directly in kind. But this lies to a certain extent outside the scope of this report. On the other side of the sexual coin. male adolescents and young men are drawn into tourist areas. attracted by the prospect of relationships with female tourists. who will reciprocate with gifts and a taste of middle-class existence. But once again. no direct prostitution is involved.

Street workers
The category of street workers appears in our sample of school children with less frequency than some others. and yet we feel that it is the most important in this report. In the streets of Kingston. one is constantly aware of two types of child workers. These are the newspaper sellers and the wipers of windscreens who can be observed in groups at almost every busy street intersection and in many plazas. The overwhelming majority

of these are boys, aged from eight to 15 years. They are poorly clothed, frequently barefoot, dirty, and undernourished. During the period of fieldwork several government schemes with the object of investigating these children's lives and alleviating their situation were in force. Not all of the schemes were successful, and we felt that the reasons for this were similar to the reasons why the education system is unable to deal with the problems of absenteeism in schools. In both cases the schemes were inclined to be inflexible and attempted to insert the child into a system of pre-existing rules and behavioural constructs rather than adjusting to meet the needs of the child and the conditions of its existence.

Although wiping windscreens is seen as tantamount to begging and therefore in contravention of the Juveniles Act, it is one of the most common forms of street labour.

The boys wait until traffic lights have stopped a stream of vehicles and then dash amongst the cars to wipe windscreens and wheedle small amounts of cash from the drivers for this 'service'. In the morning and late afternoon newspaper boys join the group busily dodging the traffic. There is a great deal of competition, both individually in getting to a particular 'client', and between groups of boys who operate from different pitches. Within these groups, older boys also prey upon younger ones. This takes two forms, either they terrorise smaller boys and steal the money they have earned, or else they have a semi-monopoly over the cloths used for cleaning, and take a percentage of the smaller boys' earnings. Danger comes from both the traffic and from within the workforce. At the time of fieldwork, several boys in the group which we studied were involved in street accidents, although not all of these actually happened on the pitch. Possibly because of the casual attitude they developed to traffic, the boys were also in the habit of travelling to and from 'work' by hanging on the backs of buses. According to one boy's report, a 15-year-old was killed when he fell from a bus after the driver had tried to shake him off. Fights within and between gangs are frequent and, as most of the boys carry some kind of sharp weapon, the injuries can be severe. One voluntary worker described the fights to us as 'vicious' and added that the cuts to which he attended almost daily were often serious knife wounds 'not just little scratches'. We saw for ourselves the scars (which many small boys carried on their faces and bodies) as evidence of the hazards of their mode of gaining a living.

The boys can usually manage to wipe two or three windscreens when the cars stop 'and then the lights change for we'. Payment varies. The replies from nine of the boys who were asked about their earnings indicated that these varied from 2 to 3 dollars in an hour and a half to 10 to 15 dollars in a four hour afternoon period, to 10 to 30 dollars a day of which 5 to 6 dollars were given to parents.

It should be remembered that these boys are not only illiterate and functionally innumerate, they are also to a large extent inarticulate. By this we do not mean simply that they speak a broad form of Jamaican creole which renders much of what is said in the world around them inaccessible, but also that the language and vocabulary which many of them have at their disposal renders much of their environment conceptually inaccessible. Their knowledge of the world is limited to such an extent that many of them do not know the names by which they are formally registered, some seem simply to be known by nicknames. They are thus particularly badly adapted to make sense of a formal education. When they are forced into school they have a tendency to abscond, to return to the life they felt they understand. But if they do this after they have come to the attention of some formal authority, they are likely to be labelled as delinquent. Whether or not the cash income is actually necessary to their immediate survival (and the boys made it clear to us that in some cases it was not), the acquisition of immediate cash to fill immediate needs was their priority. Money is the central and most accessible means they have of making sense of their world.

The rehabilitation scheme which most impressed us was an experimental guidance programme sponsored during the early part of 1980 by the Kingston YMCA and the Canadian High Commission. This operated a free school which the boys attended as and when they wished. Those who did attend on any one day would disappear en masse around five o'clock when the evening rush hour traffic began to build up and earnings could be expected. An important part of the scheme was the introduction of discipline. The boys were dirty and undernourished and often in need of dental and medical attention. A condition of being able to use the YMCA swimming pool for instance, would be that a boy had washed beforehand. They were encouraged to take a pride in their appearance, to clean their teeth and take care of their bodies as part of the requirement for attending classes. The scheme, and the form of education which it offered, were adjusted to the boys' perception of their own needs. A car wash scheme was started for visitors to the YMCA on Saturdays. This gave the boys extra income, took them off the streets and was the starting point for simple mathematics, when the day's takings had to be counted and shared out. The project organisers stated that, during lessons, these children were capable of learning only from a strictly concrete situation, they were so tied to the idea of immediate return that theoretical subjects were outside their grasp. But, at the end of three months, there had been some progress; some were able to do simple computation and others could write their names and even spell a little. But, more importantly perhaps, it was reported to us that the boys were 'able to be more relaxed about money, to think about other things'.

It is extremely difficult to be precise about the home circumstances of these children. Most came from a slum area in West Kingston, where they lived in government-built tenements. Most came from mother-headed families with seven or eight siblings. But household composition varied and did not always include all the siblings. Some older brothers and sisters would be 'in the country', others 'in Miami'. Sometimes a boy would mention a father, but might state that he had not seen him for some months because 'him busy'. Another boy, who said that he lived with his father, then admitted to sleeping in the park 'a whole heap of them live down there'. Family and household composition seemed to be loose and perpetually shifting. One mother we spoke to was neat, intelligent and well dressed, but she had recently been abandoned by the man with whom she had lived in a consensual union for most of her adult life. Perhaps because of the difficult conditions of her own life, she seemed to lack control over her ragged and independent child. The organisers seemed to think that it was quite common for parents of these proto-adults, in the midst of the struggle for survival in the urban ghetto, virtually to lose interest in their children. One boy stated that his father

> don' stop mi from hustle, because . . . mi can't depend on mi mother, so mi mus' work if see way (what) little mi can earn miself fi (for) mek life.

And another said of hustling that 'it better for wi than wi go thief'. In some cases the child's earnings were clearly an important contribution to household income; like the small boy who seemed to be supporting his mother and pregnant 13-year-old sister, or the nine-year-old living in a nuclear family who claimed that his parents sometimes beat him to make him go out hustling on the streets. But his stated contribution to the family income was small. He earned five or six dollars a day, of which he only gave a portion to his mother. The way the boys spend their own share of their income varies also. Some use it to buy food; most gamble and some smoke ganja. But an important aspect is the independence which it entails.

> The highest ah (I) mek one day is $2 and mi put it to good. Mi give mi mother half of it to buy plate and the rest for mi pocket money and the . . . same that when school open I can have fi mi lunch money.

It is unlikely that these intentions to go to school will be carried out. All the boys we met were either non-attenders or sporadic attenders of formal schools, even though they would all confidently claim that they would return to school 'on Monday'.

Newspaper sellers can more regularly earn money and to a certain extent the activity is institutionalised. Theoretically at least, the work can be fitted into a school day, although, in our experience, it tends not to be. Children obtain the papers from dealers, who purchase from the newspaper publishers in bulk. The boys we knew, simply said that they obtained their supplies from 'a man name Winston'. This wholesaler thus obtains an income from the boys' activities. Sometimes a wholesaler will be a parent of one or several of the children. The newsboys purchase the papers directly from the wholesaler and keep the resale profit. We were unable to ascertain the wholesaler's earnings from this trade, but the boys said that on Fridays they would take about $15 (the paper cost 50c) and this would mean that during the weekday $7.50 or less would be a good day's takings. At Christmas they would expect $25. Actual take-home earnings each day would be around $3 to $5. For this they would have to sell between 150 and 200 papers. Thus a wholesaler supplying five boys would have an income of about $50 a week, after paying for the papers. The paper in question, *The Star*, which is the evening sister paper of the *Daily Gleaner*, Jamaica's oldest newspaper, encourages sales by organising 'Starboy of the Year' competitions.

The Medical Social Work Department of the University Hospital reported on the conditions of work of these children in 1978. An approach was made to the management of the *Daily Gleaner* to see if an hour's schooling a day could be provided as a condition of the newsboys' employment. Management refused, and was reported to have stated that it was 'not responsible for children's literacy'. Since then no action has been taken. It would seem unlikely that such an approach would work since the newspapers are sold in bulk to dealers who, in turn, sell them to the newsboys.

Windscreen-wiping street boys appear to graduate to selling evening papers. The morning papers were sold by older boys, usually in their late teens. Exactly what happens to boys who become too old to wipe windscreens and sell newspapers is one question we cannot answer at this point. A boy over 15 can no longer use his youth, which was virtually his only saleable asset, to wheedle casual coins from motorists. Given the ghetto setting of his home, his uncertain household circumstances, the general unemployment in his neighbourhood and his own lack of skills, his future is almost certain to remain within the limitations of the casual sector, where the highest returns are bound to be in criminal activities. Unless he is lucky enough to come into contact at an early stage with one of the few government and quasi-government self-help rehabilitation programmes which have a good success rate within the slum areas and which teach some practical skills and provide some employment opportunities, his future is bleak. And unless unemployment in Jamaica is considerably reduced in the immediate future, it is difficult to see how these schemes can be expanded.

Multiple labour

Until this point, we have tended to treat the various categories of labour as if they are mutually exclusive. But among the most important aspects of survival strategy among the poor and unemployed are adaptability and flexible self-reliance. Just as the family and household are entities which shift in composition according to economic circumstances, so the individual is constantly seeking opportunities for cash income from a variety of possible sources. Every economic niche, however small, is assiduously mined for whatever return it can bring. A category of person frequently referred to in the press, literature and political rhetoric is the 'sufferer', the deprived and disadvantaged. In some cases, the appellation is derogatory. The 'sufferer' is referred to as if he or she is wallowing in misery rather than trying to improve the conditions of existence. But the sharpest impressions remaining after reading the childrens' essays were of the strength and will to survive exhibited by children who did not want to be unemployed or turn to crime. Many had clearly adapted to multiple forms of labour, in an effort to obtain an income and improve their situation. The following essays, by a girl and boy, both in their mid-teens, are simply two examples of the variety of modes which can be taken up, and of the determination to make the most of life.

The girl wrote:
When I am not in school I comb hair like braids for two dollars I cook and clean wash or do some knitting in the days in the evening I go to bible class and sometimes I play games like baseball table tennis and I sell gums on weekend I sell one for ten cent and go to visit my grandmother and father and my friends and we all go fishing and I go to the farm to farm vegitables and yam banana all kind of food and fruits when I am not in school I try to do plenty thing to help at home because we all want money to spend clothes to wear food to eat and if we dont try we cannot make life we cannot depend on our parents alone we must can make it with out them by buying things like gums, oranges, sweeties, and by making things for our self like I do when I am not in school sitting down not help us we can work to help our self when I say work I just means to make your hone (own) things to sell – buy things to sell hew (how) I see when I am not in school.

The boy wrote:
When I am not in school I do a lot of things sometimes I go to taylor shop and do some pressing to get some money to come to school and when I am not pressing I am at the shoe marke (maker's) shop and helping the shoemarke man fix shoes and the man gave me money so I do all sort of job to help myself to school because my mother cant afford to send me to school because she have a lot of small child and I am the fifth one and my father inst (isn't) supporting we becaus he is not working so I have to work for myself. sometime I even go to sea but I dont like going there because it is too dreadful and too

much fishermen die out there. but if you want to reach the top you have to come from the bottom. but I know that some day I am going To be something in life but I still enjoy what I do. and this is when I end my Composition.

4 Conclusions and recommendations

Most of the wide variety of work undertaken by Jamaican children, and as shown in this report, is found in the casual sector of the economy. Some children do work in the formal sector, usually on an informal basis. Their wages, rates of pay and conditions of work are largely unregulated and, consequently, they are vulnerable to exploitation. In the casual sphere, children work within the household, often so that their mothers may be free to earn a living and, in addition, many work in a variety of street jobs in which conditions of work are injurious to health and impair physical and intellectual growth. Because of the responsibility thrust upon Jamaica's children and the self-reliance and independence they develop as a result, many of them grow up before their time. They become proto-adults adept at surviving in the midst of poverty and unemployment.

Radical improvement of the child labour situation cannot be effected without fundamental economic and social changes aimed at eradicating poverty. Without such changes it is difficult to see, for example, how unemployment may be reduced or how the state will be able to provide the welfare services which could enable households to survive without utilizing child labour either at home or outside. Nevertheless, the situation of child workers could still be improved considerably if certain commonsense actions were taken. None of these suggestions require major legislative changes. They do not entail large economic investments. Nor do they depend upon alleviating the overall economic difficulties of Jamaica, or stemming the present level of violent crime. But what they do need is a change of attitude, and a shift of priorities, so that institutions are produced in a form appropriate for the children they exist to serve.

It is recommended:

That the government of Jamaica

(a) adopt a more flexible attitude in respect of education policies to allow children to combine school-attendance with part-time or seasonal work;

(b) re-appraise the requirement of compulsory school uniform in state schools;

(c) re-inforce and improve record-keeping methods in schools so that the children's progress and welfare can be monitored despite frequent changes of house and school;

(d) Provide additional community-based nursery and creche facilities by:

(i) strengthening the present structure of informal sharing of child care between women through encouragment of official child-minding and some welfare and financial support;

(ii) providing nursery and creche facilities for the under-fives at schools, thus enabling older children to attend school with the younger siblings left in their charge;

(e) include the 'free school' methods (as practised by the Trafalgar Street Boys Project) in schemes for the rehabilitation of street workers;

(f) review and amend the relevant legislation in order to end the discrepancy between the minimum school leaving age and the minimum age for admission to employment.

Appendices

Data from schools
(a) *The Sample*
Jamaican social studies usually divide the island up into four types of area: Metropolitan (meaning the Greater Kingston area plus the north-coast town of Montego Bay). Urban. Rural and Deep Rural which are rural areas with very limited contact with towns because of poor road transport. These categories reflect environmental amenities rather more than employment amenities. Thus we divided our sample into five categories: Metropolitan (as above). Urban. Urban Tourist. (towns in the north-west tourist area. where hotel employment is available). Rural. including Deep Rural. and Suburban (Rural areas which have easy means of commuting to a Metropolitan area).

The sixteen schools in our main sample were selected from the four parishes shown on the map. The proportion of children studied in rural areas appears small. but this reflects the constraints of time and difficulties of travel within Jamaica. Rural schools are often difficult to reach. even by car. and the number of children attending each school is usually small. It should also be remembered that these figures reflect only the areas in which the schools were situated and that many children travel from rural areas to attend school in towns.

The sixteen sample schools were in the primary, all-age and secondary categories, as it was judged that the incidence of child labour was likely to be greater where the opportunity for educational advancement was less. But it should be noted that high drop-out rates have also been recorded for some high schools. The majority of children in the sample (61 per cent) were students in secondary schools (age range 12 to 17); 25 per cent were from all-age schools (age range five to 17) and 14 per cent from primary schools (age range five to 11). Where possible. we selected schools which, as far as we knew, had not been the subject of previous research.

The main sample of 2,025 children aged from eight to 17 is about 0.3 per cent of the Jamaican population in the total age group. We also examined data from 98 children in the five to seven age group from one rural all-age school. Because schools vary greatly in size, we were unable to select the same sample number of children from each school. This was because we wished to examine all ability ranges, as well as children in both shifts in schools using the shift system. Thus we requested data from all children in the selected grade who attended school on the day when data was collected. This also avoided teacher-bias in selecting 'good' pupils. It also meant that in some cases blank data was collected from wholly illiterate children. This accounts for the 121 invalid cases in the computer sample.

(b) *Data*
Four types of data were collected from each school.

i) an assessment of the school itself from both official statistics and observation.

ii) Texts of extensive, unstructured interviews recorded in written form with head teachers, work-experience teachers, guidance teachers and individual class teachers. Informal interviews were preferred to formal questionnaire methods because of the small number of schools and the great variation among them in terms of size, type and location. In addition, as we suspected, unstructured interviews tended to reveal a great deal of information on subjects related to the inquiry but of the existence of which we had previously been unaware.

iii) Attendance rates were collected for each school for the first day of the school year in 1979, and two weeks in 1980, one of which was chosen because it was at a time of severe food shortages. Because school records are kept in different ways it proved difficult eventually to collect this data. Nevertheless it was possible to produce Figure 2 and some data on drop-out rates is being collated for a longer report. (See Preface).

iv) The main research data was a collection of essays on the topic 'What I do when I am not at school', written by the children for their usual teachers and in normal school time. This method was preferred over questionnaire forms of data collection for several reasons, principal among which was the judgement that a free essay might be more revealing than direct questioning, as well as giving a more qualitative insight into the children's lives. The results were amenable to content

62

analysis via computer, as well as to literary appraisal. In the coding of essays prior to computer analysis, we tried, where possible, to err on the side of under-estimation. Thus any dubious cases were coded as 'no labour' or 'not known' particularly in the case of domestic labour. Essays were of course obtained only from moderately literate children enrolled in and attending school. In addition, as children were writing the essays for teachers, they might be inclined to repress their involvement in some means of gaining an income. It can thus be seen that the figures we provide are most likely to be an under-estimation of the problem.

Tables 3, 7, 8, 9 and 10 were derived from cross-tabulation of the elements selected for coding from the essays. Further tables will be discussed in a subsequent longer report. It is worth noting that high degrees of significance were found in all cross tabulations.

Other data

1. Unstructured interviews were recorded, in writing, from a large number of academics, social workers, lawyers and government officials. From many of these people we were also able to obtain statistical data.

2. In order to gather data from drop-outs we made contact with a government sponsored scheme to help unemployed youth in the slum areas of Kingston, and had discussions with some of the organisers as well as some of the 13 to 17-year-old boys involved. The boys then used our tape recorder to interview each other, in our absence, about their life histories, present situation and aspirations. The tapes were transcribed and copies of both tape and transcript given to the organisation involved.

3. A similar procedure was followed with the eight to 15-year-old street boys taking part in the Trafalgar Street Boys Project. In this case the interviews were made for us by the project organisers, who also gave us the data they had collected from the boys and their families for the purposes of their project.

Appendix 2
Tables

TABLE 1

Youth unemployment

	April 1977	April 1978
Labour force		
Employed	902,000	918,170
Unemployed	221,700	212,200
Unemployed rate		
Total	24.6	23.1
Male	16.1	13.2
Female	34.8	34.7
14-24 years age group		
Total	44.6	43.5
Male	32.0	27.5
Female	60.3	61.5

Source: D Powell, *Some Social and Demographic Data on the Jamaican Youth,* 1980, ISER, Kingston, p. 10.

TABLE 3

Primary reasons mentioned for absence from school by children in sample

---

Reasons	*Number of mentions*	*Percentage*
Illness	69	59
Lack of lunch money	22	19
Lateness	15	13
Weather	8	7
Friday absence	2	2
Total	116	100

Note: lack of uniform was mentioned by several children but only in a secondary capacity.

64

TABLE 2

Attendance rates at selected secondary and all-age schools in sample week beginning 7 February 1980

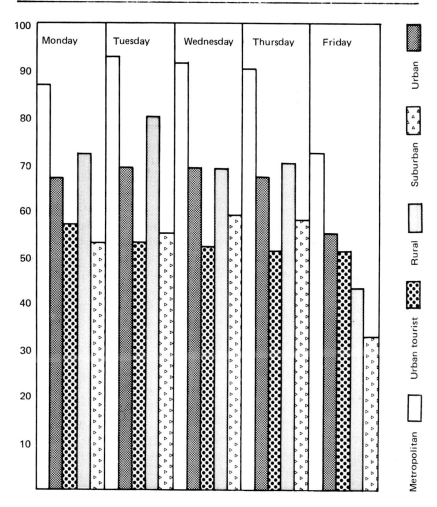

Note: It is a general pattern that Friday is the day of greatest absenteeism in all schools. This is partly because it was previously a day on which schools were closed. But many children remain at home on this day to help a higgler parent or guardian to prepare for market or to care for younger siblings while an adult goes to market.

65

TABLE 4

Reasons given by Jamaican school principals in primary and all age schools for children's absence from school

	Metropolitan		Urban		Rural		Remote rural	
	Rating	Rank	Rating	Rank	Rating	Rank	Rating	Rank
Clothing	4.8	4	6.0	1	5.1	4	4.3	5
Home duties*	5.3	2	4.1	5	5.8	1	5.6	1
Food	5.1	3	5.6	2	5.5	2	4.6	4
Travel	3.5	7	3.0	7	2.6	7	3.3	7
Child care*	5.9	1	4.6	3	5.4	3	5.1	3
Work*	3.8	6	4.4	4	4.1	5	5.5	2
Illness	4.3	5	4.1	5	3.4	6	3.4	6

(*These categories would all be included as child labour in the present report).

Source: The causes of student absenteeism as perceived by primary and all-age school principals, with their suggested targets and strategies for improving attendance. Report prepared by the Research Section of the Ministry of Education (Jamaica) 1979.

TABLE 5

The 14 to 19 age group in the labour force

Date	Employed			Unemployed			%
	Male	Female	Total	Male	Female	Total	Employed
October 1977	36,000	10,600	46,600	27,100	38,400	65,500	41.57
October 1978	41,300	11,500	52,800	29,500	42,300	71,800	42.37

Sources: 1977 Abstract of Statistics; 1978 Economic and Social Survey

TABLE 6

Categories of work engaged in by Jamaican schoolchildren in sample (Grades 4-11)

Category	Number of cases	Percentage of sample
Not known	121	
Definitely no labour	1,383	68.30
'Work'	20	0.99
Part-time or weekend	33	1.63
Holiday work	10	0.49
Apprentice	49	2.42
Shops	18	0.89
Manufacture	7	0.35
Farming	173	8.54
Parent assistance	27	1.33
Parent substitute	9	0.44
Child care	36	1.78
Domestic	200	9.88
Vending alone	18	0.89
Vending assistant	33	1.63
Hustling	2	0.99
Fishing	7	0.35
Total	2,025	100.00

Note: 'Parent assistance' indicates help with a parent's own paid work or help in a family business, excluding household labour and street vending.

'Parent substitute' indicates substituting for a sick parent or one otherwise unable to work at paid employment, so that the employment is not taken up by another adult in the parent's absence. 'Vending alone' indicates a child selling in the street independent of an adult, usually selling its own produce or products.

'Vending assistant' indicates a child who helps an adult vendor, possibly by helping to mind the stock, or alternatively by helping to obtain the goods.

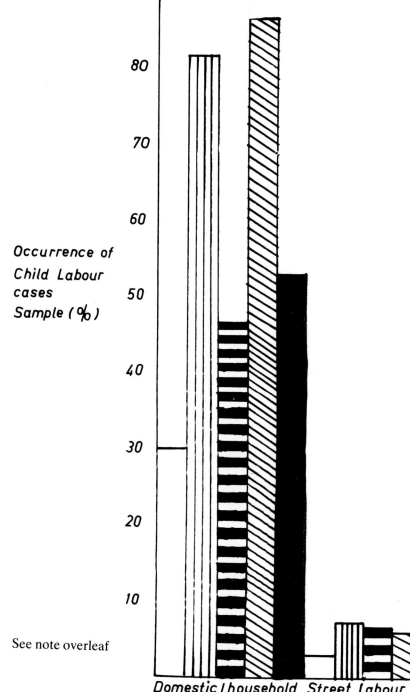

TABLE 8

Occurrence of
Child Labour
cases
Sample (%)

80

70

60

50

40

30

20

10

See note overleaf

Domestic / household   Street Labour
(includes farming)

OF LABOUR BY AREA

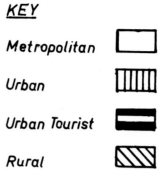

KEY

Metropolitan

Urban

Urban Tourist

Rural

Suburban

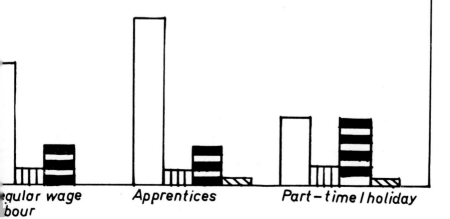

Regular wage
labour

Apprentices

Part-time / holiday

Note: Too few children were involved in fishing to be included here.

All types of urban areas have higher incidences of labour than rural areas, except in the household category which includes farming. This urban bias reflects the greater employment opportunities in towns. The exception is the surprisingly low occurrence of street labour in metropolitan areas. We believe this is because metropolitan street workers, particularly from slum areas, are usually early school drop-outs and will therefore not be represented in our sample. This was confirmed by the information we collected from street boys in Kingston.

The very high percentage of street labour in the suburban sample reflects the children's involvement in helping to sell rural produce with parents at weekends. The suburban areas border on, or are surrounded by, farming areas and have good transport connections with the metropolitan areas. As these tend also to be areas of smallholdings, the households are particularly well situated to provide the town market with fresh fruit and vegetables.

(This note relates to Table 8)

TABLE 7

Labour by school type

School type	Total known cases	Number in sample	Percentage of child labour cases
Primary	285	103	36.14
All-age	500	138	27.60
Secondary	1.240	401	32.33

Note: The greater percentage of labour performed by primary school children is probably an indication of the number of children who drop out of school all together at about the age of 11 after failing the 11-plus test. These children will then be integrated wholly into the casual labour force and will not appear in the sample of post-11-plus school children.

TABLE 9

Known household composition of children in sample

	Number	%
Nuclear	241	22.0

Female-headed

	Number	%
Mother alone	27	2.5
Grandmother	23	2.0
Aunt	31	2.5
Possible mother alone	668	61.0
Total	749	68.0

Male alone

	Number	%
Father alone	7	0.5
Grandfather	5	0.5
Uncle	13	1.0
Possible father alone	74	7.0
Total	99	9.0

	Number	%
Foster or guardian	5	0.5
Child alone	3	0.5

Appendix 3
The Juveniles Act (1st July, 1951 as amended to 1975)

Part VIII. *Employment of Juveniles*

70. In this part –

'Employment' means employment in any undertaking, trade, or occupation, carried on for profit or gain, irrespective of whether the employment is gratuitous or for reward;

industrial undertaking' includes –

(a) a mine, quarry, distillery or brewery, or a sugar, spirit compounds, match, soap, cigar or cigarette factory, or any undertaking in which articles are manufactured, altered, cleaned, repaired, ornamented, finished, adapted for sale, broken up or demolished or in which materials are transformed, including ship-building and the generation, transformation and transmission of electricity and motive power of any kind, but shall not include any agricultural undertaking;

(b) construction, reconstruction, maintenance, repair, alteration or demolition of any building, railway, tramway, harbour, dock, pier, canal, inland waterway, road, tunnel, bridge, viaduct, sewer, drain, well, telegraphic or telephonic installation, electrical undertaking, gas work, water work, or other work of construction, as well as the preparation for or laying the foundation of any such work or structures;

(c) transport of passengers or goods by road, air, rail, or inland waterway, including the handling of goods at docks, wharves, airports and warehouses but excluding transport by hand;

'night work', means work in an industrial undertaking during any portion of a period of eleven consecutive hours including the hours of ten o'clock in the evening and five o'clock in the morning;

'ship' means any sea-going ship or boat of any description which is registered as a British ship and which is habitually used only for voyages from one port to another in Jamaica.

71. (1) No child under the age of twelve years shall be employed, save as is provided by subsection (2).

(2) A child under the age of twelve years may be employed by his parents or guardians –

(a) in light domestic, agricultural or horticultural work;

(b) in any prescribed occupation:

Provided that no child under the age of twelve years shall be employed in night work or in an industrial undertaking.

72. No juvenile shall be employed – Restriction of employment of juveniles.

(a) if under the age of fifteen years, in any industrial undertaking; or in or upon any ship, other than a ship where only members of his family are employed; or

(b) if under the age of sixteen years, in any night work.

73. Where any person is employed in contravention of any of the provisions of this Part, any person to whose act, default or representations the contravention is attributable shall be guilty of an offence against this Act. Responsibility for contravention.

74. If it is made to appear to a Justice that there is reasonable cause to believe that any of the provisions of this Part or of any regulations made thereunder are being contravened with respect to any person, the Justice may by warrant authorize any constable to enter any place in or in connection with which such person is, or is believed to be, employed, and to make all necessary enquiries therein. Search warrant.

75. (1) No person shall employ, for reward or otherwise, any boy or girl under sixteen years of age in or about the feeding or working of a sugar mill. No child under 16 years old to be employed to feed a sugar mill.

In any prosecution for contravening the provisions of this section it shall not be necessary to prove the age of any boy or girl employed; but if such boy or girl appears to the Justices before whom any person is charged with employing him or her, to be under sixteen years of age, the burden of showing that he or she is above the said age shall lie on the party accused.

(2) Every constable, and every person having special or general authority for the purpose in writing, from the Commissioner of Police, may at all reasonable times enter any premises whereon is any sugar mill and inspect the mill, and where it appears to him that any person feeding the rollers is under sixteen years of age may inquire into the age of such person.

(3) Any person contravening any of the provisions of this section, or refusing or neglecting to comply with any requirements made under authority of this section, or obstructing any person in the lawful exercise

of the powers given by this section, shall be liable, on summary conviction, to a penalty not exceeding ten dollars, and on a second or a subsequent conviction within twelve calendar months of a previous conviction to a penalty not exceeding forty dollars.

76. Nothing in this Part contained shall be deemed to apply to the exercise of manual labour by any juvenile under order of detention in an approved school or by any juvenile receiving instruction in manual labour in any school.

Appendix 4
The Anti-slavery Society submitted a report of its research findings on child labour in Jamaica to the Seventh Session of the United Nations Working Group on Slavery (10 August – 14 August, 1981, Geneva). The recommendations included in this report are as follows:

In view of the economic circumstances in Jamaica it is unrealistic to envisage the eradication of child labour other than in the long term. Nevertheless the situation of working children could be improved by a shift in priorities whereby facilities and institutions are developed to serve the needs of the children concerned and suit the cultural character of Jamaica.

It is recommended

1. that the government of Jamaica

   (a) adopt a more flexible attitude in respect of education policies to allow children to combine school-attendance with part-time or seasonal work: and in respect of the rehabilitation of street workers which would accommodate a voluntary schooling and training programme.

   (b) approach UNESCO to assist in regard to the above.

2. That this report be sent to ILO, WHO and UNICEF.

Anti-Slavery Society Reports

Child Labour Series

Report No. 1
Child Labour in Morocco's Carpet Industry
71 Pages. 1978. ISBN 0 900918 06 3
£1.00 (US$2.00).

Report No. 2
Child Labour in India
by Sumanta Banerjee
46 pages. 1979. ISBN 0 900918 07 1
£1.00 (US$2.00).

Report No. 3
Child Labour in Spain
by Susan Searight
56 pages. 1980. ISBN 0 900918 09 8
£1.00 (US$2.00).

Report No. 4
Child Labour in Thailand
by Sumanta Banerjee
64 pages. 1980. ISBN 0 900918 13 6
£1.00 (US$2.00).

Report No. 5
Child Labour in Italy
by Marina Valcarenghi
96 pages. 1981. ISBN 0 900918 12 8
£1.00 (US$2.00).

Human Rights Series

Report No. 1
Western Sahara: the fight for self-determination
by John Gretton
53 pages. 1976. ISBN 0 900918 04 7
75p (US$1.50).

Report No. 2
Equatorial Guinea: the forgotten dictatorship
by Suzanne Cronjé
43 pages. 1976. ISBN 0 900918 05 5
75p (US$1.50).

Report No. 3
Eritrea: Africa's Longest War
by David Pool
78 pages. 1979. ISBN 0 900918 08 X
£1.50 (US$3.00).

Also available:
Child Workers Today by James Challis and David Elliman in association
with the Anti-Slavery Society. 170 pages including 17 illustrations.
Quartermaine House. 1979. ISBN 0 905898 06 0 £3.50 (US$6.00).

Anti-Slavery Society Reports are available from:
Third World Publications
151 Stratford Road. Birmingham B11 1RD
England.
Cheques payable to Third World Publications

The Anti-Slavery Society for the Protection of Human Rights is a long- established international organization which works for the eradication of slavery and servile forced labour and on behalf of indigenous peoples whose identity and way of life are threatened.

The Anti-Slavery Society investigates, exposes and seeks to abolish chattel slavery, traffic in persons, debt bondage, serfdom, exploitation of children, servile forms of marriage, persecution of indigenous peoples and other gross violations of human rights, irrespective of the country or political and ideological system in which these occur.

The Anti-Slavery Society pursues its aims by means of comprehensive research, sending missions to countries where human rights violations are reported, publishing reports, lobbying governments and the United Nations and, when diplomacy fails, informing the international news media of such abuses in order to bring worldwide pressure to bear on the states concerned.

The Anti-Slavery Society is independent of all national, governmental, political, economic, religious, racial and ethnic interests and groups.

The Anti-Slavery Society has consultative status with the United Nations Economic and Social Council and promotes observance of the Universal Declaration of Human Rights, the 1956 UN Supplementary Convention on the Abolition of Slavery, the Slave Trade and Institutions and Practices Similar to Slavery, as well as the 1930 Convention of the ILO on Forced Labour.

The Anti-Slavery Society is a registered charity with an international membership. It is financed by voluntary contributions from its members and by grants from charitable foundations. Its headquarters are in London, England.

The Anti-Slavery Society was formed in 1839. An integral part of it is the Committee for Indigenous People, a descendant of the Aborigines Protection Society, founded in 1837 and merged into the present society in 1909.